ATROPOS PRESS
new york • dresden

Sovereignty in Singularity

Aporias in Ethics and Aesthetics

Gregory Bray

Think Media EGS Series is supported by the European Graduate School

ATROPOS PRESS
New York • Dresden

151 First Avenue # 14, New York, N.Y. 10003

cover design: Hannes Charen
cover art: Nadine May Lewis

ISBN 978-0-9831734-9-6

Dedication

This document is respectfully dedicated to my family, friends, colleagues, professors, teachers, and those who have inspired me to be part of rethinking the cyber realm and media.

I would like to acknowledge my advisor Dr. Wolfgang Schirmacher, whose Homo-Generator and Artificial Life so eloquently opened the space for me to explore. I would also like to acknowledge the professors at the European Graduate School in Saas-Fee, a living heterotopia. Barbara Hammer, Martin Heischler, Colum McCann, Sandy Stone, Carl Mitchum, Sigrid Hackenberg, Michael Hardt, Judith Butler, Slavoj Zizek, Giorgio Agamben, Avital Ronell, The Brothers Quay, Alain Badiou, Michael Anker and all the thinkers and innovators who have contributed to the university.

I would like to acknowledge my peers, in particular Amber Scoon, Sharif Abdunnur, Jamba Dunn, Anthony Gow, Sean Smith, Dara Zadikow, and Laura Long. Each have contributed in so many ways it is difficult to articulate them in a single statement. Thanks also to my colleague Dan Schackman, Ph.D., for helping give voice to the later chapters. And to John Ebert, who assisted with the final edit of this document.

Also, to my brother John, who is a devout Levinas-ian and assisted with additional research. And to my wife, Nadine, and our children, Eamon and Nora—for their patience as Daddy hid to read research and write. I owe you my entire education.

INTRODUCTION: On Singularity and Sovereignty

Following Agamben, we can say that the sovereign's basic lawmaking and lawbreaking power is the proclamation of the state of exception, the suspension of the rules. The sovereign decides whether the normal state of affairs is in effect taking place. Derrida, on the other hand, would say that the sovereign is marked by her ability to forgive the unforgivable, an act Schirmacher deconstructs by claiming that one can only forgive oneself. If Schirmacher is right, what follows is that the sovereign is only sovereign over herself.

–*Hospitality in the Age of Media Representation*, Christian Hänggi

Sovereignty as a Model for Singularity

In a sense, the following document may be considered Fine Arts as a role model for digital communication in the coming singularity. It is through the work of the artist that we can see homo generator in action, the birth of self in the space of uncertainty and singularity. This is getting ahead of the argument, though, as the terms need to be defined.

In consideration of what he calls "the coming singularity," scientist and philosopher Ray Kurzwei's latest graphs show that technology's breakneck advances will only accelerate — recession or not (Kurzweil, TED). "Information technology is growing in an exponential manner and is not linear." In invoking Moore's law as a paradigm, Kurzweil tells us that "Information Technologies (of all kinds) double their power (price performance, capacity, and bandwidth) every year." Vernor Vinge, a pioneer in conceptualizing the singularity concept in the realm of science and technology breaks it down to a simple definition:

- There may be developed computers that are "awake" and super-humanly intelligent. (To date, there has been much controversy as to whether we can create human equivalence in a machine. But if the answer is "yes, we can", then there is little doubt that beings more intelligent can be constructed shortly thereafter.) [1]

- Large computer networks (and their associated users) may "wake up" as a superhumanly intelligent entity.

- Computer/human interfaces may become so intimate that users may reasonably be considered superhumanly intelligent.

- Biological science may provide means to improve natural human intellect. (Vinge)

Kurzweil tells us that Moore's paradigm will become obsolete in 2020, and that a new paradigm will emerge. What will this paradigm be? What can it be? How will it affect our encounters with one another, our understanding of self, self-generation, in the uncertainty of singularity?

Folded into this consideration is the charting of DNA data—identity not only in the realm of what Judith Butler may call performative sexual identity, but tactile identity—which in-cludes physical traits of the body from muscle tissue to sex organs. Though these statements read like breakthroughs in understand-ing just how information technology is linked both with human evolution and human history, it has within it an echo of Donna Haraway's Cyborg Manifesto, in which she prophesized a similar scenario through her "blasphemy." Part of the paradigm shift, away from Moore's law and into a new evolution of bodily living through technology (Schirmacher, 1994) must include the under-standing of our self as a sovereign entity.

---

1   Look no further than 'WATSON,' the computer that participated on Jeopardy during the late winter 2011.

Kurzweil has achieved, in his articulation of what the 'Coming Singularity' may look like, a kind of celebrity. Articles, essays, books, and films have been made that further explore this new non-paradigm paradigm. For example, theorist and science fiction writer David Brin suggests that there are four broad categories in which singularity may emerge: the first is Self-Destruction—different forms of self-destruction from social collapse amounting to 'ecological suicide.' The second is Negative Singularity—this is the *Terminator* or *Matrix* scenario— in which self aware technology destroys the human race as a virus, a kind of mass matricide. The third is Retreat. In this scenario, we see the embrace of the neo-luddite. Specifically, the neo-ludditic understanding that moves away from utilizing technology for any purpose, and toward a more so-called 'natural world.' Throw out our toys, they are destroying us. Finally, there is the Positive Singularity, which implicates human survival, sustainability, newly practiced ethical encounters, and newly appreciated aesthetics. The following document argues for this latter form of singularity.

This is not to say that it is entirely Pollyanna. While Paul Miller argues that 'future generations will not have a dependence on technology, they will have technology as a core aspect of their existence,' the nature of existence in ethical encounters and aesthetics requires exploration.

Kurzweil makes a number of assumptions, some predicated in a surface reading of philosophy, and others using mathematic extrapolations that may presume too many conditions without variables. There is a hidden leap of faith in his thinking that human behavior exists simply as a pattern without natural variation and deviation—this does not necessarily hold together. In addition, by the assumption that the human-technological condition may hit critical mass, Kurzweil is neglecting our current communication and aesthetic interfacing, which suggests that the singularity is not only coming, but is already here.

For the last two generations, at least, we have been part of the birth pangs—as evidenced in our information technology and aesthetics. Some of these pangs have not been pleasant. So the central question then becomes: if we are experiencing the birth pangs of the next human evolutionary step using technology as an interwoven vehicle and developing organs toward this next step, how do we learn more efficiently what we are capable of in ethical encounters, what aesthetic begins to emerge, and as we are creating this next evolution ourselves, how do we then recognize the role of sovereignty outside of governance in the offline world?

The first argument this document makes throughout is that we must recognize ourselves as a sovereign entity. A sovereignty of self in the singularity. While this concept, the notion of sovereignty in the singularity, does look at the positive singularity, at the moment of its creation we can see its opposite taking hold in some of its birth pangs—these moments, the case studies that I look at in the document such as Stacy Johnson, Megan Meier, and Kevin Sites, are cases that this theory must own, accept, and then grow stronger with. Sovereignty in the singularity is about the fluid aporetic, with an ability to adapt and move inside a Hegelian second negation.

In Samuel Weber's paper, *Toward a Politics of Singularity*, he takes on Hobbes, beginning with the treatise, *Leviathan, of The Matter, Form, & Power of a Common-Wealth Ecclesiastical and Civil*. In contrasting notions of protection and obedience, he brings out the phrase "of which the condition of human nature and the laws divine…require an inviolable observation" (Weber, 2009 P.7).

Through this lens, he offers that the purpose of this Leviathan is to give protection and defense of natural man "in his vulnerability" (Weber, 2009, P.7)

In thus emphasizing the object of his treatise as being nothing other than setting "before man's eyes the mutual relation between protection and obedience," Hobbes closes the circle of the work that began by describing the purpose of the Leviathan as that of assuring "protection and defence" of "natural" man in his vulnerability. (Weber, 2009, P.7)

The protection, Weber continues to extrapolate, is a bureaucracy that protects itself in order to protect those that this body intends to serve. Weber, in his examination, poses a key question: "in what does the protection consist? Who is to be protected from what?"

And here, Weber makes an argument, which one can trace through Adorno and into post-modernity. This is the failing of both The Enlightenment, and what is called 'The Rational Man'. Leviathan is the artificial body, the corpus without, and yet the principle of this governing grows into sovereignty. Hobbes' conception of life is immanence, and yet gives sovereignty over to a body—the Leviathan itself, since only as long as it thrives can the "lives of its individual members be assured."

The principle of life, as Hobbes defines it, is that of immanence: "Life is but a motion of limbs, the beginning whereof is in some principal part within." If it is to be a living body, Sovereignty is thus determined by Hobbes as "an artificial soul" capable of "giving life and motion to the whole body." The "whole body" here of course is that of the body politic, which includes its various elements, human and non-human "magistrates, and other officers of judicature and execution" which Hobbes compares to the "joints" of the artificial body, wealth and riches: its strength, *salus populi* (the people's safety) its business and finally, "pacts and covenants" said to resemble "that *fiat*" by which God let there be light—and created the world. (Weber, 2010)

Thus, the sovereignty of the subject is dislocated by an experience of the indefinite singularity. Hobbes employs the metaphor that a limb cannot behave as such without the health of the whole body, and that the whole body is dependent upon the limbs. But is this not a total surrender of authority, responsibility, and above all *sovereignty* to a non-entity? If, as Hobbes describes , sovereignty is dependent upon the immanence of life, is the individual not a sovereign?

Sovereignty, then, cannot be a silo. The transition must go from a closed system to an open system. For Derrida , the act of forgiving came from the sovereign—the greatest form of openness is to forgive or pardon the unpardonable act. The act of forgiving, then, requires openness, as does sovereignty.

In Derrida's essay *Aporias,* (Derrida, 1993) he deals chiefly with the "rhetoric of death," beginning with a conversation on Diderot's *De la brievete de la vie.* The first step in his examination is one of truth, property, absolute property, and borders. Here, he poses the question whether truth is finite, or even finished? (Aporia) He asks, then, if it is finite what goes beyond the border, as it's clear that something else must exist in reference to truth; if it is to be confined, then is something else confining it?

> ...a rhetoric of borders, a lesson in wisdom concerning the lines that delimit the right of absolute property, the right of property to our own life, the proper of our existence, in sum, a treatise about the tracing of traits as the borderly edges of what in sum *belongs to us [nous revient],* belonging as much to us as we properly belong to it. (Derrida, 1993, P.1)

This becomes immediately applicable to space in our key arena for information technology discourse, the cyber-realm. Is it truly confinable? Are identities confinable in cyber-space? What can occur without demarcations as understood in hierarchal or hegemonic structures? Can the shifting and uncertain paradigm, and the Aporia in cyber-living, move us into a territory of différánce (Deleuze) or heterotopia celebration (Foucault)? Can information technology's speed foster inter-cultural understanding either through the simultaneous deconstruction and formation of identity, that which we immediately bring to/keep from the cyber-realm? These kinds of considerations go to the heart of who we are in *artificial life*, what inner agencies we can command and bring forth.

In describing these terms, Wolfgang Schirmacher's philosophy of Homo Generator, and on bodily living in the cyber-realm will come into play throughout. This philosophy tells us that we are self-generating, self-creating, self-birthing, and that this possibility of the creation of self plus the manufacturing of negotiable terrain (Homo Faber) does not betray the cyber-netizen's sovereignty.

Being Through the Cyber-Realm as Poros and Aporia

The cyber-realm, the fusion of information technologies and imagination, is a space that we are in constant negotiation with, which includes all the considerations of *sein,* specifically *dasein* and *mitsein* as terms given to us by Heidegger.

The demarcations that have already been prescribed in our off-line lives can exist in either terrestrial, ontological, political, or even physical (biological) lines brought into the cyber-realm—here we have the conundrum of this space. For on the one hand, we can see this space in terms of our identity. What we're capable of is nothing short of aporetic openings, embracing the, as Michael Anker would say, " ethics of uncertainty" (Anker, 2009) situated as interaction. On the other hand, there are the usual trappings of identities and identifiers (and at times those in *cultural studies* who wish to reassert their presence—not as a way of celebrating multitudes and multiplicity, but simply as critique without solution).

Language comes into play, as well, beginning with binary language: simply the one and the zero, the *virtual monads,* which moves us past media literacy. This idea of a virtual language, a simple binary system used through quantification with the zero as the *off state* and the one as the *on state* immediately alters perception of language as such—there are no phonemes.

Other than the symbol for no/thing and the symbol for one thing can the virtual be divided up? To believe there is an end to anything is where deconstruction begins. What of *virtuality* "beyond the zero?" Where does the definite article come from which allows for "the" zero? There is nothing that remains tactile, and yet can anyone deny that this realm, a realm of being and of consequence, is not categorically *real* and reshaping the way we as the cyber-netizens experience the world as we know it? All windowless monads are virtual wholes comprised of elements which reflect and contain the whole while being themselves comprised of monads. The elements are made of elements, which are made of elements, etc. and the wholes are virtual[2].

A division of one and zero in this binary language indicates a relationship between something and nothing. The zero can only be as *off,* can only be as *nothing,* if the one were to be *something.* Zero, One, zero, one, zero, one. (What happens, then, when *two* is introduced?) Consider this, then, not an evolution of language per se, but the next phase of being in the cyber-realm, where any traditional division, even that of language as a tool of segregation, no longer needs to be applicable in sovereign encounters.

---

2   I must thank Jamba Dunn, doctoral student at the European Graduate School, whose yet-to-be-published research examines virtuality and monads in a breadth that this document will not.

What then, of bodily tactility in these interactions? The body is ever present in the cyber-realm, in terms of both texture and aesthetics. Indeed, if we are in the state of apoiesis, if we truly are homo generator, then we are in constant negotiation between synthesis, synthetic, and aesthetic creation. Being-becoming as self in multiplicity and with the other in the same space.

In order to properly address the questions, the terms of the dialogue need to be defined, and the text that follows takes a stab at it. The first part defines the terrain. The second chapter discusses in greater detail the first part of this introduction: that is, what is the sovereignty of self? How is self a governing agent in the cyber-realm?

The third chapter, On The Politics of Death in the Cyber Realm, will discuss loss, as understood through Freud and also Deleuze, while bringing in Heidegger's Being For Death. Here the case studies will include Megan Meier, who took her own life as a result of a MySpace dialogue, as well as remembrances that extend in the cyber-realm well beyond where the physical body has ended.

The fourth chapter, On Journalism Ethics in the Cyber-Realm, asks a basic question about journalism: what does it mean to bear witness as a journalist in the singularity? Where are the ethics, or notions of professionalism, located? Who do we surrender our authority to when we allow another to bear witness for us? Whose account matters?

This blends into the fifth chapter, On Crossing Cultures in the Cyber-Realm, which discusses case studies of the self as journalist, as the self bearing witness and giving account of actuality, through intercultural communication in the cyber-realm.

The third part of the book, divided into two chapters, looks at 'Homo Generator Aesthetics as a Role Model for Singularity'. The sixth chapter begins by moving past the adult entertainment industry to explore eroticism, aesthetics, tactile pleasures and fulfillment in the cyber-terrain. Lewis Mumford, Barbara Hammer, Judith Bulter, and Wolfgang Schirmacher will address sexual identity aesthetics, and the technological embrace and orgasm. What is sexuality in the singularity? What are the aesthetics?

The seventh chapter, On Homo Generator Aesthetics in the Cyber Realm, discusses Homo Generator and the Sovereign Cyber Netizen, explorations of Carolee Schneeman's work, and finally the Life Technique for the sovereign cyber-netizen. The work of Wolfgang Schirmacher will have a strong thread throughout this work, as his notions of Artificial Life and Homo Generator are vital in order for this text to have life.

While his theories will be present throughout, they warrant a chapter on its own, to discuss Schirmacher's philosophy, and how it operates in the cyber realm.

And here, we enter the confusion of cyberspace. What is sovereignty of identity, identities, and how it shapes our understanding of aesthetics in the cyber-realm? Can fidelity exist in virtual representations, or is the very concept of representation rendered obsolete by the Heideggerian essence of this realm? Can one truly became a Cyborg, avoiding the trap of co-modification?

If we are to consider the post-dated term "information superhighway," the image of a space of limitless knowledge, limitless dialogue not bound by the time lag of letter writing, not bound by an audio experience (for one can Skype in lieu of the telephone), and not bound by any hierarchal institutionalized structure of who can access what at what time, then we are truly considering a space that gives us the possibility of a utopia, of true democratic choice, of a space where humanity can communicate to the point of reaching a greater potential than we have in past generations.

These questions only begin to approach the meta-questions surrounding this misunderstood terrain, the space of our coming singularity, and this document will return us to what Slavoj Zizek and

Alain Badiou believe the chief responsibility of the philosopher is: to point out that the right questions are not being asked, and to reframe the conversation (Badiou & Zizek 2009). Or as Schirmacher says, paraphrasing Habermas, "It cannot be the task of philosophy to render meaning" (Schirmacher 2003).

PART ONE: Sovereignty in Singularity:
Its Formation and Negotiation with its Opposite

Chapter One: On Ethics in the Cyber-Realm

Cyber Living at the "End of Modernity"
The Fall of Goliath, The Rise of Singularity
Essences Toward Ethics

> *In the most general sense of progressive thought, the Enlightenment has always aimed at liberating men from fear and establishing their sovereignty.*

> –Horkheimer and Adorno

> *The Boundary between the physical and non-physical is very imprecise for us.*

> –Donna Haraway

Cyber-Living at the "End" of Modernity

What are the concrete issues in perfecting our lives, and how can the cyber-netizen bring the self into this necessary role for creating a space for ethical encounters, and bodily living? Wolfgang Schirmacher suggests that we cannot, "after all, enforce a change in human behavior, it must be discovered" (Schirmacher).

If this is true, then how has technology served to foster both our change, through our own actualization, our own sovereignty, and how can we see the *essence of technology* (Heidegger) as a means for putting to rest destructive commodification forces? Are those forces even still relevant?

While ethical paradigms exist, (and yes this text will ultimately draw upon several), the difficulty as Wolfgang Schirmacher tells us, is to find these paradigms implemented, put into action, in such a way as to affect real change in our behaviors. A question to ethical encounters is in order, not just encounters as they pertain to otherness, encounters within us, encounters with nature, and encounters in virtual spaces—the cyber-realm.

For Schopenhauer, the self exists in relation to the factors around it. For example, the concept of "status" in a society behaves as a destructive force to the self. For Adorno and Horkheimer, the self existed in a social web of delusion. Others have located the self as in relationship to the contextual demarcations around it—the self is the self in relationship to the terrain. *Where am I?*—in relation to *Who am I?* Who can we be in the singularity?

Where are we, both in history and in our cyber-terrain? Let's begin this passage, then, with the end of modernity, in its relationship to mediated technology. Max Horkheimer and Theodor Adorno trace the evolution and destructive forces of *the enlightenment* as modern thinking grew through the Industrial Age. A single question regarding the enlightenment emerges: what went wrong? The term suggests, among other things, a desire to push against institutionalized models of power—that which commodifies (Marx and later Adorno with Horkheimer) for consumption traditions, and beliefs, through the marketing of simulated desire. Yet, if one were to trace modernity, the industrial revolution, and the Enlightenment led to World Wars, and wastes produced as a byproduct of the Industrial age on a scale so massive generations ahead will feel the poisons we have all left behind. The effects of this age were real, and still are real, for many of us today. Is there any doubt that the BP oil spill, which went far longer than necessary, is a reminder of modern capitalistic thinking? Consider the 'Rawstory.com' article, which pointed out that a solution was tenable. The solution would not allow for any of the oil to be accessed again, so the spill continued. After all, to the corporate-minded, saving the oil and converting it to riches was the key drive in solving the problem, not avoiding the larger environmental disaster. (Webster, 2010) Or the failings of the nuclear power plants in Japan after the devastating tsunamis? Modern rationality?

The cultural industry, that part of it which still has some presence and attempts to exert its will through media, politics, and business—is the result of what we can see in some areas of contemporary thinking--*libertarian reason.*

The emphasis on *Reason*, as Theodor Adorno has suggested, either masked darker humanistic leanings, or lead directly to what he called 'a new barbarism.' It was in fact these periods of thought that predated, linearly, some of the darker moments in recent Western history.

What of the reaction against it? Part of the folly, as echoed by Wolfgang Schirmacher and again by Martin Hielscher, was the *institutionalization* of a utopian ideal—creating a power structure in reaction to a previous power structure. This kind of idealism, as Nietzsche has argued, can lead to a form of totalitarianism, where there must be adherence to the new-fangled idea, at risk of being marginalized, ostracized, or even at the risk of violence. Even the reaction *against* this form of reasoning is problematic, as it lead to new and equally dangerous political and social structures. To Adorno, rationality treated as universality, limited the individual to repressed compliance (Butler, 2005, P.4). Not to mention that once the new utopian ideal was institutionalized it immediately becomes part of the structure it fought. Alain Badiou suggests that the problem of a revolution is that when it succeeds it becomes the enemy it fights. (Badiou, *Politics without Politics*)

In examining the era that lead to the post-modern condition, a simple truth must be put forth: the human condition can do better, and is capable of far greater, and part of this involves shedding the pre-existing structures as they relate to our particular culture regime in mediated technology. The hierarchy, that which privileges those at the height of this order, must be brushed aside. *Being* in the cyber-realm, then, must push against what Martin Hielscher calls misjudgment in privileged knowledge:

> the gesture of privileged knowledge, or insight, the viewpoint that fancies itself lofty and shrewd, in confident awareness of its opposition to a sea of ignorance and blindness, is still a viewpoint that has not broken with the self-misjudgment upon which the false world rests, a viewpoint that is not even aware of its self-misjudgment (Hielscher, 2003).

Here, Hielscher is crystallizing Adorno's concerns, chiefly experienced in *Negative Dialectics*, and in *The Dialectic of Enlightenment*, co-authored with Horkheimer. The larger idea is the democratization of information, learning, theory, technology—knowledge. Modernity has ended, but its consequences have not.

Moving past modernistic understandings of self caught up

in systemic webs, one has to consider not only the post-modern conditions of cultural apparatuses, but also of the "where am I" in relation to mediated technology development into the singularity. At its core, though, the essence of being and identity, which includes that kind of experiential learning, social factors in the creation of *I,* and a push past what R.D. Laing has called *The Politics of Experience,* or what is considered normal in the face of a variety of experiences (though Laing pushed against the binary considerations of normativity and mental illness) in the face of social, industrial, and cultural changes is at its core a call to pursue *the good life.*

The cyber-realm, as "techno-enthusiasts" (Nakamura, 2002, P.2) have purported, then opens the door for raw experiences of identities without modernistic confines. In order to give form to our modes of thinking empathy and *openness* must be ever present. In this consideration, the cyber-realm must drive the conversation as the philosophical and virtual terrain. In this, there must also be a word on *cyber-types,* perhaps the next stage in socio-semiotic reading of demarcation (before a necessary negation)—but before we have *types* we must have terrain, the realm.

A quick clarification on how to define 'the cyber-realm'— it contains the traditional Internet—grown in part from Advanced Research Projects Agency Network (ARPNET) credited as being the first packet switching network as developed by the United States Department of Defense. Though this is often credited as being the initial stab at the internet, it also includes alternate forms of information technology: consider the early attempts at television, which transmitted over the telephone lines, before tower-transmission was possible. In fact, in 1927 the earliest experimental television program was transmitted by telephone wire from Washington DC to New York City. This was "final proof that commercial broadcasting was technologically feasible" (Stracynski, 1996, P.8). In other words, the early attempts by Vladimir Zworykin (who held the patent on the iconoscope camera tube, the predecessor of the cathode-ray tube), and other television pioneers created an early version of the internet, and the technology would remain somewhat non-vital until decades later. The cyber-realm refers to the World Wide Web and all of the addresses one can visit. It also refers to virtual reality, and other virtual spaces where a user not only manipulates an identity or an avatar, but *is,* in part, *being* through avatars and a multitude of identities in a bodily experience (here, it is less as a representative symbol, and more as a purified identity, in a multitude of identities,at times a sum of parts, at times parts without the whole). It is in these virtual interactions where the seeds of the new dialogue exist—non systemic, non-hierarchal, and non-institutionalized. The germination of these seeds is at this point another matter.

The twenty-first century has seen the rise of a truly new mediated landscape, with social media *tools* (Heidegger, though this word may be too limited, as Schirmacher asserts that technology is the flesh of our flesh) such as Facebook, Twitter, Second Life and Four-Square, while also giving a new birth to cultural interactions in cyberspace. This space can be thought as an inter-space, or a liminal space (Mulvey) free of the confines of other mediated forms, and (for now) free of the institutional censorship put upon us by the FCC (Privacy is another issue, which will be touched upon later). It is at once technological and organic. "The computer is our organ, and not our tool" (Schirmacher, 1989).

As the academy continues to wrap its "technocratic" (Zizek, 2006) vision of curricular adaptation, it has introduced a series of catch phrases, attempting to make dogmatic that which is untenable. Yes, we have heard the word 'convergence,' as a means of explaining to media studies students that what they do now is to act as producer, director, distributor, and consumer (at times the term 'Pred-i-tor,' a pejorative/acronym of Producer ,Director,

Editor)—an interactive force in the cyber realm. This term, however, has its limitations—for rather than embracing a new democracy in liminal spaces, it attempts to ideologically fuse together pre-existing platforms, bringing the baggage of television, email, film, radio, etc. along for the ride (Lacan). In her book, *Cyber Types: Race, Ethnicity, and Identity on the Internet,* Lisa Nakamura begins by asserting that a new language, a new way of seeing, is in order.

It truly does call for a re-conceptualization of media studies, and constitutes a call for new terms more appropriate to "software studies" to convey the distinctive features of new media, in particular the use of the computer. (Nakamura, 2002, P.2)

Here, Nakamura was drawing upon *The Language of New Media* by Lev Manovich and Espen Aarset. She could have very well drawn this from earlier texts by Baudrillard and Schirmacher, or even Deleuze. The point remains: rather than treating the space as something truly new and exciting, to explore identities, processes (Deleuze and Guattari, 1972, March 1983) it is being treated as a logical evolution of pre-existing mediated spaces, an argument that simply must be refuted. The emerging cyber-culture is New (capital N new). It brings to light possibilities of intercultural interaction, democratization of media, and adds another nail into the coffin marked Theodor Adorno's Culture Industry (Its death, as Schirmacher has argued correctly, was telegraphed by the emergence of the Music Video).

Disappointingly, Nakamura falls back into the grasp of cynicism, embracing *problematicing-as-social criticism,* as opposed to phenomenology—which requires reporting only at once what is in front of her.

Critical theory itself, which she is quick to simultaneously glean from and refute, provides some of her terminology of distancing—but she glorifies cyber-typing, "identity online is still *typed,* still mired in oppressive roles even if the body has been left behind or bracketed" (Nakamura, 2002, P.2).

The body is not left behind in the cyber-realm. One lives through their body. Whatever enhancements may exist, they exist as new organs, and not as a replacement parts. All senses are heightened when in the cyber-realm—tactile, emotional, and psychological. Body factors into bodily-living. We live through our processes, our metabolism, our thoughts—well past Descartes' *cogito ergo sum*. Hans Jonas put some of these thoughts to bed decades ago in his work, *The Phenomenon of Life,* where he traced human evolution beside mediated evolution. We have self beyond any epistemological-historical sense of self, and beyond the scripting we surrender our authority to. In his review of this work, Ezequiel Di Paolo contends that:

> For Jonas, a goal-seeking machine is still far from being a value-generating machine, its purposes are derived and do not feed back into its constitution. It remains to be seen whether artificial intentionality is impossible short of building a fully metabolizing system or whether there is an alternative in the understanding of how non-metabolic values originate. Cybernetics and artificial intelligence have not seriously taken up this challenge but the sounds coming from new disciplines such as autonomous robotics seem appropriate. (Di Paolo, 2001)

Nakamura puts forth other ontological concerns, and some will be addressed in later chapters, especially in framing the self in the cyber-realm. The ethical encounters push against a philosophy of limitations and embrace one of openness. Remember that *philosophy* in part speaks to what we are capable of, and not how things *should be* according to a single voice. The singularity then means plurality.

> There is no meaning if meaning is not shared, and not because there would be an ultimate or first signification that all beings have in common, but because meaning is itself the sharing of Being. (Nancy)

In *Becoming Singular-Plural* Nancy has stated that there is no existence without co-existence, and that being does not come before being-with. Therefore, we are being with the world, being with each other, being with in intra-personal communication, as well as with the technology—no longer allowing any aspect of it to become an overlord or a tool of control by another outside of ourselves.

The Fall of Goliath, The Rise of Singularity

If the culture industry itself is broken, beyond the means of carrying on its production, and truly fractured, it will fall apart. When the edifice crumbles, democratization of media and identity will truly have a strong role in shaping our experiences without mediated-authoritarian influences.

An immediate example is the advent of the mp3. This music file became a conundrum for the music industry. With this file, compact discs were no longer the popular format for music consumers. Take into account that music is a youth-driven industry (as for example, Justin Bieber, The Jonas Brothers, and Hanson before that). In the 90s, youth purchased music on compact disc. Earlier, the audio tape, while the vinyl recording struggled to not disappear into storage media obscurity, like the 8-track or the mini disc which failed to 'cross the chasm' (Moore, 2002). In his work *Crossing the Chasm*, Geoffrey Moore described in detail categories of 'innovators' and 'early adopters' of new technology. In this work, he discussed technology that had crossed 'the divide' between what the public was willing to buy, and what had been discontinued, or fell into 'the chasm.'

Take into account the 78s, the Victrola, and all other recording devices that now reside in museums. What they have in common is the tactility of the reproduction, which Walter Benjamin was so eager to celebrate (his text, *The Work of Art in the Age of its Technological Reproducibility* [Benjamin, 2008 edition] remains a forerunner to 21st Century mediated conditions) toward the end of modernity (Schirmacher). With the mp3 there is no storage media outside of a portable hard disc and minimum software for a traditional mp3 player. It is simply a transferable file. A disc without a groove, ridge, a still frame, or anything tactile. It exists as zeros and ones.

This tiny innovation of technology has completely altered the music industry: the goliath that has for decades generated the culture-of-cool, as the late music critic Lester Bangs had correctly asserted decades ago (Derogatis, 2000). According to recent research, 11-16-year olds access music via download, as opposed to purchasing a physical disc (Rixham, 2010). I-Tunes has attempted to offset the democratization of music with single song services at a low price, but it is fighting with torrents, streams, and even the ability to create mp3s from audio present on YouTube music videos. The music industry has had to adapt, but still has not yet recovered (Rickybains1, 2010). The music is now in the hands of the people, not of the industry.

We can see a similar trend occurring in television. Online web content from Hulu, to sites of *questionable* legality from tvshack. net, ninjavide.net, and other sources have negated the need for 'appointment viewing' in television. It should be noted, in terms of these latter two examples, that they are third party steaming portals, and are at this time not viewable. In the summer of 2010, the authors of the sites have been held responsible for material they stream, an abrupt turn of face from previously understood legal distribution matters. Their argument, that they do not store any of the information, and simply act as a third party portal collecting the information, seems to be, at the moment, no longer legally viable. Technology moves faster than our laws. No matter. Shortly after being taken down, new domain names appeared performing the exact same function—the streaming media outlets evoke the image of a multi-headed hydra. Cut one head off, and two will generate in its stead.

A viewer selects exactly what she wants to watch, when she wants to watch it, and often *where* she wants to watch it as well. From the computer monitor to small mobile devices, the television programmers are now in a situation where they must adapt, or fall apart.

Niche marketing, such a catchy concept not more than ten years ago, is next to fall victim to the cyber-realm. Rather than being able to safely box groups of people into various categories so that Neilson can show mathematical abstractions (soft data) to manufacture household numbers for advertisers (hard numbers from soft data), the cyber-netizen has total control over intake, output, and dialogue. The Nielson methodology for advertising approval is simply a mirage, and has been for quite some time, using mathematic estimates to suggest 'young people like *xyz* ,' 'old people like *abc*,' and we're going to put the word 'blacks' into a box, and deduce that twenty-percent of all blacks in America are turned on by *efg*, and so how do we get more of them tuned in? This is nothing short of propagandistic planning, and a form of nihilism—reducing human beings into a numeric abstraction. As Adorno and Horkheimer have said of this practice, the public is catered for with a hierarchal range of mass-produced products of varying quality. Thus advancing the rule of complete quantification. Everybody must behave (as if spontaneously) in accordance with his previously determined indexed level, and choose the category of mass product turned out for his type. Consumers appear as statistics on research organization charts, and are divided by income groups into red, green, and blue areas; the technique is that used for any type of propaganda. How formalized the procedure is can be seen when the mechanically differentiated products proved to be all alike in the end. (Horkheimer &Adorno, 1969, P.123)

This modernistic practice is facing a forcible end. The individual cyber-netizen decides what she wants when she wants it, Neilson and the entire antiquated system of driving advertising dollars be damned. Neilson figures, now more than ever, are a mutually shared illusion between network executives and advertisers, and nothing more.

The cyber-realm, along with the DVR, DVDs and Blu-Rays mailed to the home, have seriously damaged appointment viewing television—leading network executives to embrace as many live stunt programs as possible, such as the 'Dancing with the Stars' or 'American Idol' programs—to get viewers to tune in live. The live event program, a staple of television since its advent, has returned with a vengeance. But is it too little, too late? And how long before u-stream.com, make.tv, just.tv, and other internet services that provide 'live viewing' experiences in the cyber-realm put an end to corporate-controlled digital broadcast?

Hollywood has maintained its monetary license in great part due to an investment in large *tent-pole* productions, investing more money in fewer films guaranteed to generate hundreds-of-millions at the box office. This, in part, serves as a reaction toward film audiences moving away from the theater, in favor of Netflix, bit torrents, and all the technology mentioned earlier. In order to ensure that audiences will come, they've had to bring back 3-D! How long will the fad last this time?

In other words, simple services which allow streaming such as Netflix, Blockbuster, or other subscription sites, as well as torrents and third party streaming (youtube.com, vimeo.com etc.,) as well as ancillary outlets such as snagfilms.com, have democratized cinema creation and distribution, as has self-distribution through Createspace on amazon.com, and cdbaby.net. This has the potential for providing a "culture without reverence." No "masses being deceived here, each piece of information is freely accessible and begs to be used" (Schirmacher, 2001).

Media industry giants, dependent upon larger distractions, and a bigger carnival, look at the possibility of following the music industry in a few short years. After all, once the public is entirely used to no purchase fee of media, or a simple subscription fee for a fiber optic internet cable, where does that leave the mass-cultural output?

In addition, as younger generations mature as *being* in the cyber-realm, do the other forms of 'media' now suffer in passivity? The entertainment industry will have to rethink all the old tried and true models, while the cyber-realm citizen can live in a virtual world, making minute-by-minute selections of nearly limitless mediated content. And, while not viewing it, producing it—shaping the new mediated landscape in such a way that individuals without the resources of money-money goliaths never could before.

Looking ahead and this is admittedly through a lens of positive thinking, one can imagine a grass-roots organization altering the shape of political discourse. Consider the first televised presidential debate between Senator John F. Kennedy and Vice President Richard Nixon—this televised debate, according to Donald Hewitt of CBS News, served as the actual election. "My God," he said, "we just elected a president of the United States and it isn't even Election Day!" (Gander, 2002, P.66)

Is it unreasonable to suggest that there will be a president whose popularity stems from grass-roots movements in the cyber-realm? If John F. Kennedy was the first 'television' president, then who will be the first 'internet' president?

The only limit to this paradigm is our thinking. We have been trained in passivity, and relying on previously established demarcations. We tend to gravitate toward the familiar, and labeling is helpful to that end. E-marketing exists as a way to co-opt the cyber-netizen into a variety of online stores, and attempts are made to perpetuate the kind of mediated thinking we experience in our off-line lives. Viral Marketing campaigns have become normative practice for new films, such as 42 Entertainment's work for *The Dark Knight* in 2007 through 2008, and products such as Mekanism's work for Frito-Lay in 2008, with their *nolaf.org* campaign.

Even with these attempts, there is the possibility of moving past these influencers with a decisive click. The focus then, turns toward ethical encounters and growth in the cyber-realm, moving past occasional desire.

Essences Toward Ethics

There are ethical matters for consideration when navigating through this cyber realm. After all, there are real consequences and real violence that can result from any kind of interaction. A quick Google search of issues in cyber space reveals some sparse questions that are being bandied about with regard to cyber-bullying, cyber-sex, legal issues such as intellectual property ownership, etc. Some of the blame, that which is put on technology's lap, is unfounded yet entirely accepted by some techno-journalists.

A recent study instituted at the University of Michigan suggests that college students today demonstrate 40% less empathy as opposed to students in the 1980s and the 1990s. The study did not evaluate the causes behind their findings. According to the USA Today article that covered the university study "one reason may be that people are having fewer face-to face interactions, communicating instead through social media such as Facebook or Twitter" (Steinberg, 2010).

The key researcher, Sara Konrath, went on to say that "empathy is best activated when you see another persons' signal for help" (Steinberg, 2010). This finding, of course, supports an argument put forth by Emmanuel Levinas throughout his work in exploring the *Other*. Of course, what this kind of view neglects is that genocide tends to occur during these face to face encounters, directly in front of clear and unmistakable signals for help.

What is missing from the argument is how Konrath immediately was able to move to the conclusion that social networking was to blame. How lazy the connection was immediately made, as though we should all nod in mutual agreement that the demon in the room is technology, and not larger systemic factors. This is not the first instance that such a connection between technology and apathy has been made.

Adorno refers to the culture industry, which of course is one created by and through technology, which obscures people's consciousness of themselves and of their real social situation. (Hielscher, 2003)

It has made the technology of the culture industry no more than the achievement of standardization and mass production, sacrificing whatever involved a distinction between the logic of the work and that of the social system. (Horkheimer & Adorno, 1969 p.121)

Nakamura is in agreement, and brings this concern to the cyber-realm. *Cyber-typing*, as she maintains, is a practice of bringing stereotypes or behavior interactions predicated upon racism and sexism into the cyber-realm (Nakamura, 2002). She addresses what she calls two camps: the first camp takes the *master's tools*, which does little as they are still in the master's house. The second camp hopes to destruct off-line societal behaviors by "envisioning cyber-technologies as less the master's tools than tools for discourse that can take any shape is an optimistic way of seeing things" (Nakamura, 2002, P. 30).

In the demarcation of camps and ideas, she is sadly creating an arbitrary delineation while also denying the full experience of *bodily living* in the cyber-realm—more concerned with semiotic representation and co-opting by forces outside of our own sovereignty and authority. To this idea, as well as to Konrath's report, Wolfgang Schirmacher has the most appropriate response:

This was an argument he made about bodily living with technology, a response to working against "biological tyranny," and is at its core a negation of many of Nakamura's concerns within the cyber-realm—in which the human body and response is absolutely necessary. This goes to the very center of our current living situation in and with the cyber-realm. "Modern technology is no longer derided as an opponent but rather recognized as our own present way of life" (Schirmacher, 1994).

With that said, communication will continue in this space for the foreseeable future, and the cyber-realm will continue to be a key source of engagement for populations for decades to come. Both Marshall McLuhan and Lewis Mumford contend that when a piece of technology is introduced into society, or a new conceptualization of technology is put forth, it cannot be removed, as (to them) technological determinism moves forward.

In his book, *Understanding Media: The Extensions of Man*, McLuhan made several large assertions, among them that media truly is an extension of man, that the medium *is* the message (moving beyond a simple paradigm of 'you can't separate what you say and how you say it'), and that media had turned the world into a *global village*, where we can all experience an event simultaneously, and experience shared grief, joy, laughter, etc. Some of this may be true, but McLuhan's "hard-ware primacy" (Schirmacher 1989) proved to be a short lived idea. As Schirmacher states, "the global village showed itself as an ethical world beyond the petty distinction between hardware and software" (Schirmacher, 1989), and McLuhan's push for hard-ware primacy and shared experience is immediately negated by subjectivity.

We did not *All* have the same communal reaction to 9/11 for example—individual reactions varied depending upon our country of origin, our world view, our personal loss(es), or gains as a result, and even then many experienced conflicting internal reactions to the images on the television set. If there were any lingering public reaction in the United States, one could call it a form of anesthesia—the American government was given carte blanche to react however it deemed necessary to a weary and paranoid public, alarmed by fears of what would come next.

In the United States, the reactions varied once the media-induced anesthesia wore off.   In evoking *The Dialectics of Enlightenment*, Slavoj Ziziek puts a spot-light on their conversation of medical anesthesia and chloroform.

Flourens claims that it can be proved that the anesthetic works only on our memory's neuronal network.   In short, while we are being butchered alive on the operating table, we fully feel the terrible pain, but later, when we wake up we do not remember it.   For Adorno and Horkheimer, this, of course, is the perfect metaphor for the fate of Reason based on the repression of nature in itself: the body, the part of nature in the subject, fully feels the pain; it is just that, due to repression, the subject does not remember it. That is nature's perfect revenge for our domination of it: unknowingly, we are our own greatest victims, butchering ourselves alive... (Zizek, 2002, P. 97)

Is this not, then, the closest possible experience we can have to McLuhan's understanding of the *global village*? The closest experience we can have as a 'shared' village is that of anesthesia, suspending our *real* selves and reactions to the events until after the numbing has evaporated?

In his work, *Reasons to Fear U.S.*, Noam Chomsky suggests much of the worlds' reaction can be summarized with, "'Welcome to the club.' For the first time in history, a Western power was subjected to an atrocity of the kind that is all too familiar elsewhere." (Chomsky, 2003)

Simply speaking we are not all one, single, and shared intelligence, not all one identity, not all one body. The cyber-realm, then, has allowed for the *actualization* of multiplicities (Deleuze and later Michael Hardt) in a fashion that does not organize all into a single shared entity, devoid of individualities.

When Heidegger spoke about technology (chiefly in his essay 'The Question Concerning Technology'), he used the term *essence.* "Technology is not equivalent to the essence of technology" (Heidegger, 1982). The text, at first seems cryptic, but his study is concerned with 'Being,' as an openness for 'Being.' His philosophy concerning technology and being strongly suggests that being will reveal itself in the 'very on-going of technology.³'

This calls us, then, to take a step back to look at *Being* and *Essence* in the cyber-realm. The concept of *Dasein* (or *da-sein* being-there/there-being), *In-der-Welt-sein* (Being in the World), *Mitsein* (Being-With), and also the Deleuze concept of Being *For* the World, and even Heidegger's *Sein-zum-Tode* (Being Toward Death) in the cyber-realm as essence.

What *Being* allows us to do is separate what Wolfgang Schirmacher calls 'the subject object debate,' which can open the door to a 'bodily language,' necessary for human survival in the post-modern age (Schirmacher).

This realm, then, allows for a technological and pure interaction as not seen before in any other mediated platform. It can be a stigmatized space—suffering the destructive traditions, tropes, types, co-opting, and the baggage of previous mediated experiences *if* we allow it to be so. If we admit to, and then move past, our own horizons and biases, this is the realm in which a person can truly experience their own actualization without any anesthetic, demarcation, cultural-industry control, prescribed ideological af-

3 Though one may guess whether he could have anticipated Kurzweil's understanding of Singularity.

filiation, or need for a goliath.

This is truly *the* space where a person can *be* their own sovereign, and the singularity (a difficult fusion between Nancy and Kurzweil) may ensure this.

Chapter Two

On Sovereignty in the Cyber-Realm
Giving Shape
The Avatar
The Sovereign Cyber-Netizen
On Privacy
Conclusion—Moving Beyond Models and the Truth of Self

Giving Shape

Much has been written about 'the self.' Whether considering 'the self' as situated by Michel Foucault in his writings, where he discounts the subject through his twain practices of Archaeology and Genealogy[4], or locating it in our experience of the Other, according to Emmanuel Levinas, or even going along Descartes' *cogito ergo sum*[5], or Heidegger's *Dasein*, the self, and being as such, have populated ontological journals and dialogue. 'Who am I?' is a fundamental question not only of existence, of thinking, but also of a guiding philosophical outlook.

This text, therefore, will not necessarily concern itself with some of these dialogues, nor will it concern itself with too much along the lines of identifiers and identified, though some will be

---

4   Foucault's philosophy, as it emerged and developed over time, moved from structuralism to post-structuralism—where he questioned the classical training of representation as understood as relation to object—it could only work when it operated as representation-as-such.

5   One of the most dangerous phrases in modern-thought, as it discounts being before thought.

quickly touched upon and put to bed to begin the actual discussion. This discussion is more about location of self—how *being* appears, through authority, and sovereignty. Where does one locate the self in the cyber-realm? After all, the cyber-realm betrays the traditional geo-physical, geo-political, and even geo-philosophical locations that have been demarcated time and time again. Considerations will include privacy, authority, and the avatar.

Deleuze and Guattari once wrote that "All is Process" (Deleuze and Guattari, 1973, 1982). This notion gives shape to the understanding that sovereignty and identity are in fact "process". The rather large ontological statement will give shape to understanding sovereignty as process, self as process, even *Dasein* as process. Deleuze resisted trappings of dialectics, and at times pushed against Heidegger, yet the notion of being and process remain entwined in identity realization in the cyber-realm.

The experience of self for the cyber-netizen builds upon Wolfgang Schirmacher's work, most specifically in his formation of the homo-generator, as well as bodily and art-fully living in artificial life.

The Avatar

The avatar arises after a deconstructive look at identity (Derrida). Oftentimes, the use of an avatar is employed, not as a representational being in the semiotic sense, but as a precinct of identity. One may say, "when I am online, I do not use my name in chat rooms, on forums, or even on social networking sites. This allows me to act however I wish."

On one hand, we may draw the conclusion that this person is acting out in ways she has always desired, but has not been able to fully realize, for fear of sullying her given name. There is a desire to almost distance herself from her own good name, as though this other *handle* is not at all part of her inner workings, but something that is simply in good fun.

A response, then, is that she could be acting truer to her own instincts, without any punitive fear of losing respect for whatever identity she wishes to put forth in her life to others. What she is missing, though, is that she is simply using her given name as a shield, and hiding behind a 'who I am in the cyber-realm is not really me' mantra—a chant that holds absolutely no truth or value. It is, at times, a truer form of self—not confined by any of the social norms previously mentioned such as the name given to her by her parents. Here she is behaving in part of her actuality of identity—a pack in a multiplicity (Deleuze and Guattari, March 1987).

The avatar is at times a nostalgic dream of self (who I should have been), a hope of self (who I could be) a realization of self (who I am), but never a distanced entity *from* that of self.

We change the visual or perceptive properties of a thing with our gaze—this is an accepted concept philosophically, an accepted concept in quantum physics, and also present in our reflection of self in our cyber-life. We alter through our mirror, our self-perceived behaviors, our 'handles,' and 'avatars.' It is not 'what we are,' but 'how we are becoming' (Schirmacher, 1994)

In his essay, *The Ecstasy of Communication*, Jean Baudrillard offers his thoughts on virtual spaces and hyper-simulation through what he called "Private Telematics":

> ...each person sees himself at the controls over hypothetical machine, isolated in a position of perfect and remote sovereignty, at an infinite distance from his universe of origin. Which is to say, in the exact position of an astronaut in his capsule, in a state of weightlessness that necessitates a perpetual orbital flight and a speed sufficient to keep him from crashing back to his planet of origin. (Baudrillard, 1987, P.128)

The cyber-realm allows us to go a step further. No longer are we traveling in a capsule, or in an astronaut suit, we are now outside of the rocket—floating without a suit. Not merely naked, but no skin, no muscle, no tissue, no bones, we are the tactile energy of our own inter-determinations, not using sovereignty as a demarcation, but as a mosaic of pluralities engaging in sensual tactility, all desire, all processes, and still very much in our own being.

For Baudrillard, alienation means illusion, but also this difference between inside and outside; so the problem of desire means we have an excess. Communication replacing alienation, there is no longer heterogeneity, only homogeneity.

"Now" Baudrillard asserts, "is the reign of hyper-reality." To Baudrillard, all is and can be communicable and there is no "separation of the inner and the outer...":

> Here we are far from the living-room and close to science fiction. But once more it must be seen that all these changes - the decisive mutations of objects and of the environment in the modern era - have come from an irreversible tendency towards three things: an ever greater formal and operational abstraction of elements and functions and their homogenization in a single virtual process of functionalization; the displacement of bodily movements and efforts into electric or electronic commands, and the miniaturization, in time and space, of processes whose real scene (though it is no longer a scene) is that of infinitesimal memory and the screen with which they are equipped...the real itself appears as a large useless body...
> (Baudrillard, 1987, P.128-9)

The limit Baudrillard encountered here, was the lament of a displacement of the real for the simulacra, and the simulated experience—the reproduction with no original. What he discounts, perhaps not intentionally, is the notion of bodily living in the cyber-realm (Schirmacher.) After all, the senses are all required, if not at their most acute, when operating in the cyber-realm.

One can enumerate the immediate physical processes, eyes on the screen, ears toward speakers, fingers on the keyboard, hand on the mouse (sometimes, *one* hand on the mouse—to be discussed at a later chapter), with all psychic sensors moving from one 'window' to another. Virtual reality and bio-technics provide a literal transfusion of this, compounding the argument against simulated living, toward bodily living. All bodies being transformed into movement toward openness.

Nakamura simultaneously accepts this premise, but then challenges the Deleuze/Guattari notion of multiplicities and packs:

> Chosen identities enabled by technology such as online avatars, cosmetic and transgender surgery and body modifications, and other cyberprostheses are not breaking the mold of unitary identity but rather shifting identity into the realm of the "virtual," a place not without its own laws and hierarchies. Supposedly "fluid" selves are no less subject to cultural hegemonies, rules of conduct, and regulating cultural norms than are solid. (Nakamura, 2002, P.2)

But does this not consider avatars and handles moving beyond geographic constraints? Can we not take into account that we lose any identifiably described barrier, matrix, or web—the "biological tyranny," and politics as understood in our walking world, beyond simulation and as actuality in the cyber realm? Look then, at international politics, in particular the recent Iranian election— again keeping in mind the earlier note: *we change the property of a thing with our gaze.*

A recent Washington Post article attempted to *clear the air* regarding Twitter's role in the 2009 Iranian elections (Ahmadinejad against Mousavi in a hotly contested election...to say the least). Many activists around the globe set their 'TWEET' times to correspond with Iranian time—and then began tweeting locations of opposition meeting points, and where the opposition was voting en masse.

For a time, the techno-press grabbed hold of this, and cele-brated the power of the individual in Iran, and coined *The Twitter Revolution in Iran*. The article states,

> But it is time to get Twitter's role in the events in Iran right. Simply put: There was no Twitter Revolution inside Iran. As Mehdi Yahyanejad, the manager of "Balatarin," one of the Internet's most popular Farsi-language websites, told the Washington Post last June, Twitter's impact inside Iran is nil (Reed, 2010).

The disillusionment resides in the desire of the Twitter mar-keters. This, after all, was supposed to be shaping the world! *What went wrong?*

This, of course, is not the right question. The question then, is simply, if the *tweeted* dialogue was not taking place inside of Iran's borders, where was it taking place? The cyber-realm knows no na-tional borders, does not respond to a single force, cyber-netizens are aware of the world in which they live, outside of nation-state boundaries, and are willing to share information, as well as short arguments and platitudes about politics *foreign* to their own.

Marketers may see this as a defeat, but social scientists and philosophers may take comfort in a kind of offline-world aware-ness spreading through the cyber-realm.

The marketing backlash continues:

> To be clear: It's not that Twitter publicists of the Iranian protests haven't played a role in the events of the past year. They have. It's just not been the outsized role it's often been made out to be. And ultimately, that's been a terrible injustice to the Iranians who have made real, not remote or virtual, sacrifices in pursuit of justice. (Reed, 2010)

But is this not proof positive of human interest in events

outside of their own prescribed borders, and geographic demarcations? Of humanity stepping up through technology to affect change? Walter Benjamin celebrated technology outwitting the bourgeoisie sense of art, while there is simultaneously no substitute for face to face communication. And yet, here we see the new communication operating across borders, hyper-aware in its own hyper-reality in the cyber-realm and in the walking-world. In discussing hyper-reality, Baudrillard stated "in place of the reflexive transcendence of mirror and scene, there is a nonreflecting surface, an immanent surface where operations unfold—the smooth operational surface of communication" (Baudrillard, 1987). Marketers may disparage, especially those looking to capitalize in an international investment for communication technology hardware, but the human element remains intact.

The cyber-realm is a dimension that is perpendicular, and not parallel, to our own. We move through it, with other cyber-citizens as handles and avatars, in a space where we recreate ourselves.

The cyber-realm brings with it the nostalgia, the remembrance, feelings remembered and anew, and the subjectivity of identities and persona for a layered engagement. We are not only living our lives, we are also writing them, and rewriting them. It is an instant nostalgia we create in social media spaces. "Having been changed into this autobiographical 'writing,' communication can now be defined as authentic, as a responsible style of media" (Schirmacher, 1989). Our Facebook and MySpace photos, our tweets, our online presence as avatars—all rewrite our histories, all affect the political and social terrain, and create the dimension for us to exist as such. Nakamura misunderstands the role that identity plays in the cyber-realm.

Despite claims by digital utopians that the internet is an ideally democratic discrimination-free space—without gender, race, age or disability—an analysis of both textual and graphic chat spaces such as LambdaMOO, Time Warner's The Palace, and Avaterra's Club will reveal that these identity positions are still in evidence. (Nakamura, 2002, P. 21)

The misunderstanding here occurs from the generic thesis, "the mass-claim of 'digital utopians.'" There is no such thing as a discrimination free space. Part of the negotiation in the cyber-realm is encountering the limitations of our own biases based upon social, ethnic, sexual, or otherwise ideological demarcations. To suggest that we leave our biases behind in this space is invalid. To suggest others do the same is equally invalid. The negotiation of these social conflicts resides in our own sovereignty.

The Sovereign Cyber-Netizen

The recent public discourse and debate between Jean-Luc Nancy and Alain Badiou regarding international response to Libya's internal crisis has flung notions of sovereignty back into the forefront of our public dialogue. Nancy has supported outside military action, as expressed in his "What the Arab Peoples Signify to Us." This writing celebrates the uprisings in the middle-east by a young generation weary of dictatorial control, while also making an argument for international intervention on Libya's behalf. In his response, "An open letter from Alain Badiou to Jean-Luc Nancy," Badiou indicates deep disappointment with Nancy's arguments for international interference. Part of this stems from his distrust of European policy makers:

> Isn't it self-evident that Libya provided an entry for these powers, in a situation that elsewhere totally escaped their control? And that their aim, completely clear and completely classic, was to transform a revolution into a war, by putting the people out of the running and making way for arms and armies—for the resources that these

powers monopolise? This process is going on before your eyes each day, and you approve it? Don't you see how after the terror from the air, heavy weapons are going to be supplied on the ground, along with instructors, armoured vehicles, strategists, advisers and blue helmets, and in this way the reconquest (hopefully a fitful one) of the Arab world by the despotism of capital and its state servants will recommence? (Badiou, 2011)

In addition, he has concerns about Libya's independence being interrupted by outside interests:

We have to make a stand against the grain, and demonstrate that the real target of Western bombers and soldiers is in no way the wretched Gaddafi, a former client of those who are now getting rid of him as someone in the way of their higher interests. For the target of the bombers is definitely the popular uprising in Egypt and the revolution in Tunisia, it is their unexpected and intolerable character, their political autonomy, in a word: their independence. (Badiou, 2011)

The question for them both is one of sovereignty. If Libya is indeed a sovereign nation, then how can external action be justified in the face of an uprising? Yet, the question of the sovereign and sovereignty moves beyond borders. For example, if one were to live next to a house where abuse were taking place, that party does not necessarily have to get involved until she bears witness to the act. Once she has witnessed the abuse, she does have the right to intervene. The largest question, as Badiou tell us, is of motive. But a sovereign citizen or a sovereign person can take action as a sign of Derridian openness in his sovereign model.

In thinking about sovereignty in the cyber-realm, one must push back the immediate state-apparatus associated with the term. This is not the *Gedankenstaat (State in Idea)*, nor a model of surrendering to a representational power or structure in the realm of geographic or social confines. Hegel, in dealing with situations of sovereignty and representation asserts that "freedom is only possible for a people having the juridical unity of a state." In his dialectic, though, he adds that the "participation (*Mitwirkung*) of the general will in the most important matters and in those concerning the universal... freedom is unthinkable" and in consequence this institution is "today part of sound human reason." (Kerevegan, 2000)

> A person of the sovereign is henceforth thought of in terms of his function, and he himself becomes secondary in relation to the abstract essence of state sovereignty (Kerevegan, 2000)

The assertions made by Hegel above demonstrate an institutionalized understanding of sovereignty, a concept that has been addressed in countless annals of geopolitical discourse. But in considering sovereignty in the cyber-realm, and how technology drives off-line discourse through a heightened awareness of our very real world, where are the 'representatives?' Where are the nation-states or feudal apparatuses to give authority, law, boundaries, or notions of demarcations associated with this thinking? A person in the post-modern condition (Lyotard) operating in the cyber-realm is acting as their own sovereign entity, a sovereign of self. Subjectivity is a social function: one must investigate the society to understand the individual—this concept is present in writings by Michael Hardt and Guattari. In framing social function, and functionality, subjectivity and communication, otherness and openness, one now has to take into account all that is within and without the cyber-realm, but not be bound by it.

In discussing a person or an individual, one has to negotiate the person as multiplicities in lines of flight (Deleuze and Guattari), and deal with an encapsulating "person." Not that Deleuze and Guattari wish to only introduce a simple dualism: "There are only multiplicities of multiplicities forming a single assemblage, operating in the same assemblage: packs in masses and masses in packs" (Deleuze and Guattari, March 1983 P. 24). What comprises a person, then, are these packs in lines of flight through the cyber-realm.

Lyotard tells us that it is "Ethically accepted that a 'person' implies 'freedom.'" (Schirmacher and Lyotard, 2005) This freedom is to be as such, and not solely in relation to systemic structures that can provide societal damage. Nor is the freedom marginal, mitigating behavior from a precinct of our identity. As Wolfgang Schirmacher reminds us, "we bring out the whole self in virtual culture" (Schirmacher, 2001)

Recently issues negotiating privacy, identities, and behaviors have surfaced again and again, and the academy is quick to jump into this fertile academic terrain. Part of the negotiation is the concept of 'behavior,' or how one interacts in one space against another. This drive, though, stems from the notion of behaviors in context to the situation: the work-self, the at-home self, the in-town self, etc. Part of the mechanisms of behavior is the use of identity as a shield, as a way of negotiating terrain and protecting of one's own reputation.

Martin Hielscher, in discussing Adorno offers,

...for Adorno at the same time a critique of bourgeois society which deludes the individual caught within a struggle for self-preservation with the nation that he is a unique individual, while the organization of society prevents individuation (Heilscher, 2003, P. 28).

A possible failing can be seen at play in how people, especially those with any kind of power, including employers, can abuse the cyber-realm through a misunderstanding of self. In his work discussing *The Human Flaw,* Schirmacher offers:

The self can never step out of its own perspective, and everything that the mind consciously, unconsciously, or intuitively generates remains irrevocably anthropomorphic, autopoietic, and distinctively its own (Schirmacher, 1991).

We do live our lives. We just, at times, impose a simulated context as a means of fabricating meaning-production. Self becomes less evident, identities are formed, shaped, forgotten, ignored, self-created, distorted, etc. The confines of the offline-world are not part of the negotiation, even if the "baggage" (Lacan) from the world is present in the netizens' actions. The misreading of these concepts is that the identity-body is abandoned—it is, in fact, ever present.

In thinking of cyberspace, Wolfgang Schirmacher ascribes to the domain the word "Networld," though that may only scratch the surface of this domain. "World" may be too narrow a term when describing the cyber-realm. It is all at once an existence that is ours and perpendicular to ours, without the grounding of gravity or planetary pull in a larger system. It is system-less outside of ones and zeros, pervasive, invasive, without identity, or structure—paradoxically it is a (dis)order in itself—a realm not separate from, but informed by our real and manufactured experiences. It shapes us, and pulls from us who we are. It is space and time, which according to Schopenhauer, are key elements to individual sovereignty.

Thus, there are two dissimilar concepts that share a connection. First, that a person, as understood, is a free being—not 'given' freedom by any hierarchal means, but simply free as such. *Dasein* (Heidegger) is then freedom in motion. "Dasein…which translates as upon. The word itself is derived from *co-agito, agito* meaning to "set in violent motion, drive onward," and to "impel forward" (Jenkins, 2010).

Second, that this person is constantly in struggle for self-preservation, a concept brought forth by Schopenhauer in much of his writing. Schopenhauer, in the *World as Will and Representation*, almost compels the subject to extinguish itself for the true experience of nothing— though, in his later beliefs, in his 'lighter' moments, lead him to the conclusion that suicide is the confirmation of the will, and that the will—an animalistic drive that exists beneath reason, must be combated with thorough intellectual ethics[6]. And as Wolfgang Schirmacher once quipped in Switzerland, 'what is the point of being dead?'

Sovereignty does imply a power constituted by being, a law unto itself. In a sense, the law stems from the original—there is some form of law, but it adapts and pulls us out of anarchy. Lyotard offers "The law is not only respectful with regard to others, it must also be taken over from oneself in a particular way...the law regards as very dangerous a world where everything is allowed" (Schirmacher and Lyotard, 2005). The cyber-netizen, acting as her own sovereign, is her own governing body—self generating.

Throughout his work, Giorgio Agamben discusses notions of constituted and constituent power—constituent power is that which exists in all people, and the constituted power is that which is created by law to govern the populace. Aside from this distinction of authority and power, Agamben asserts that constituted power grows in strength, and defends itself against constituent power, serving as a boundary to shelve human *rights* in its own desired fashion.

Look at the 'protest pit,' common in the United States at this point. While the United States Constitution puts forth a guarantee of Right to Free Assembly, the power of free assembly is taken away by the same authority, claiming that those protesting presi-

---

6   Consider his work in *Axioms and Maxims*, where he gives a philosophy that seems strangely affirmative against his earlier work such as 'The World as Will and Representation.'

dential policies (Constituted power), must do so in certain government approved lots, under surveillance and secure locations, generally a large distance away from the main event. Leaving the pit would put the citizen in jeopardy of legal punitive measures such as arrest, detention, or even suspicion of terrorism.

How does one then negotiate the contradiction? After all, as Lyotard purports,

> we can have the feeling that there is a law there and that to instrumental-ize someone, a child for example, violates the law …We are inconsistent, and it is therefore impossible to bring about a balance and have a complete, fulfilled, happy life (Schirmacher and Lyotard, 2005).

Giogio Agamben pushes against this, with two sweeping utopian statements. First, "One day humanity will play with law just as children play with disused objects, not in order to restore them to their canonical use but to free them from it for good" (Agamben, 2005, P.104). And second that he does not believe in any systemic punitive system. (Butler and Agamben, 2009). Zizek fires back that the only systemic punitive system that could work would occur in a utopian scenario, to maintain the utopia[7].

Schirmacher has a response to them both: "I can only punish myself" (Ronell 2009). The self as sovereign asserts itself.
The second notion, that of a *sovereign entity* needs to move beyond the trappings of nation states and representation—a self is sovereign in the cyber-realm. It can neither invade, or be invaded—it simply just is as *essence* (Heidegger).

Here, the cyber-netizen, operating as the sovereignty of self must reveal its own authority, even against the rational self. Wolfgang Schirmacher evokes Freud when he tells us that "the rational self is not its own master" (Schirmacher, 1985) yet sur-

---

7   Slavoj Zizek, youtube.com/egsvideo

rendering authority and sovereignty are not the ends for a cyber-netizen living bodily in the cyber-realm. The sovereignty here is one of openness, not of hierarchy or of invasion.

Invasion deals with several ideas, but for now two come into focus: privacy and authority.

On Privacy

Wolfgang Schirmacher asks 'What right have we to conceal how we really are? Phenomenologically, the question is sound, and it pushes back against the negative associations brought forth by privacy" (Schirmacher, 1985).

In *The Human Condition*, Hannah Arendt distinguishes public and private forms of speech which belong to the public sphere and those that belong to the private domain. Accordingly, she contends that: The private domain has no speech, it is an arena in which bodies labor; defined by repetitive and transient actions; to have speech properly means it must be done in the public domain; these distinctions are based on the Greek polis but they are non-exclusionary; the public depends on the private to exist and yet this dependency is never theorized as a political issue because the public contains the private (Arendt, 1998).

In this sense, the cyber-realm is a hyper-public domain—both public and private at once. Baudrillard suggests that "in a subtle way, this loss of public space occurs contemporaneously with the loss of private space. The one is no longer a spectacle, the other no longer a secret" (Baudrillard, 1987). Our *being* in the cyber-realm allows the consummation of both the private and the public—and understanding of essence as such moving fluidly through a terrain without margins. To this concept, Wolfgang Schirmacher adds, "The long dominant difference between public and private sphere has been suspended, and the Internet has become the universal venue of encounter" (Schirmacher, 1994).

In a recent New York Times Article, "The Web Means The End of Forgetting," Jeffrey Rosen, a law professor from George Washington University, compiled research in the area of privacy and makes several claims (Rosen, July 19 2010). He provides a case study of Stacy Snyder, a then 25-year-old teacher in training who had lost her job due to a picture she left posted on her old myspace. com account—a picture of her in a pirate costume holding an alcoholic (presumably, it was in a plastic cup) beverage, with the words "drunken pirate" below the image.

She lost her certification, at the end of the exhaustive training, as the academy deemed her unworthy to be a public servant. The 'drunken pirate' was not the image the powers that be wished to purport, or subject young minds to. When Snyder sued, the Supreme Court declared that the image and text accompaniment were not guaranteed under "protected speech." From this example, Rosen begins with the thesis that "the Internet never seems to forget it is threatening, at an almost existential level, our ability to control our identities; to preserve the option of reinventing ourselves and starting anew; to overcome our checkered pasts" (Rosen, July 19 2010). He adds,

> ...for some techno-enthusiasts, the Web was supposed to be the second flowering of the open frontier, and the ability to segment our identities with an endless supply of pseudonyms, avatars and categories of friendship was supposed to let people present different sides of their personalities in different contexts. What seemed within our grasp was a power that only Proteus possessed: namely, perfect control over our shifting identities" (Rosen, July 19, 2010).

This collusion stems from a misconception in the cyber-realm. You are not representing yourself, acting as a Sausurrean symbol in a semiotic state, you are *being* yourself. What is left in the cyber-realm when all else has been stripped away? In the cyber-realm, the cyber-netizen no longer has the shield of identity. "The self is autonomous solely through autopoiesis: it is here in the endowment of successful or unsuccessful life and nowhere else that I reveal or conceal myself" (Schirmacher & Lyotard, 2005). Rosenberg's article hits these key points:

> a person who puts forth each side of their identity—the me at work, the me at home, the me at play, is susceptible to dangers of work if they step out of the moral ring of behavior.

> new software exists to help re-establish reputations of those who feel they have been damaged online through new consulting firms—always for a price, of course.

> Most people aren't worried about false information posted by others, they are worried about true information they've posted about themselves, and that is taken out of context.

> Some legal scholars want to expand the ability to sue over true but embarrassing violations of privacy.

> Facebook and other social networking sites may have 'expiration dates' for information enforced, though this scenario seems unlikely

> People tend to be themselves on Facebook; it is not about augmenting who they are, but facing consequences for who they are.

> A "humane society" values privacy.

> Digital forgiveness and empathy is possible. (Rosen, July 19, 2010)

They want control over their online reputations. But the idea that any of us can control our reputations is, of course, an unrealistic fantasy. The truth is we can't possibly control what others say or know or think about us in a world of Facebook and Google, nor can we realistically demand that others give us the deference and respect to which we think we're entitled. (Ibid)

Quite frankly, the truth is that we cannot possibly control what others say or know or think about us in any world. The demarcation of social norms between one world and another must face full eradication, as it is at this point simply arbitrary at best. The question one could post to Stacy is *why would you align yourself for an organization who does not accept you as who you are?* Why work and behave under such restrictions, when educating requires an ethical agreement between teacher and student—and the same agreement would not exist between teacher and state in this paradigm? To evoke *Paradise Lost*, find 'another enterprise' (Milton, 1918) perhaps a private school. It must be recognized that openness does have its consequences, but openness is in itself a form of passive-resistance. Only openness will guide us back toward empathy and ethics.

There are elements to be aware of as a cyber-citizen, of course. First off, there are malware programs, spy programs put forth by the government, or third parties interested in identity theft, as well as larger attempts to demarcate and seize control of the realm from a variety of authoritarian pockets concerned about true democratization. In fact, according to the same New York Times Article:

> According to a recent survey by Microsoft, 75 percent of U.S. recruiters and human-resource professionals report that their companies require them to do online research about candidates, and many use a range of sites when scrutinizing applicants — including search engines, social-networking sites, photo- and video-sharing sites, personal Web sites and blogs, Twitter and online-gaming sites. Seventy percent of U.S. recruiters report that they have rejected candidates because of information found online, like photos and discussion-board conversations and membership in controversial groups. (Rosen, July 19, 2010)

The cyber-black listing and employer practiced cyber-vetting begin and yet, openness must be encouraged. It is through openness that the larger issues, those of surrendering authority without question, giving up sovereignty, and accepting instrumentalism approaches to technocratic removal of individualization, can be put to rest. Openness is key to empathy.

Consider that there are more than 100 million registered Twitter users, and the Library of Congress recently announced that it will be acquiring — and permanently storing — the entire archive of public Twitter posts since 2006. Everything. Stored. In perpetuity.

Man may not 'ontologically need privacy,' as Schirmacher purports, but man does need sovereignty and authority that is not easily handed over to databanks for blanket causes. Identity theft and other nuisances are easily avoidable problems if one takes the time to secure against needless data-mining. It is not privacy for privacy's sake, for openness should be a condition for discourses, but paradoxically for security against personal theft—which is a logical measure. But how does one negotiate this paradox?

First, take the argument away from privacy all together. There is no objective reason for hiding ourselves. The truth is that, contrary to popular opinion, the data files on us give not a distorted but an approximately true picture of life in those areas capable of being monitored by the computer.

> According to the Phenomonological Method, how a thing reveals itself is not to be predetermined.' This is very much true. We must move past privacy, as it is then a non-issue, and to that of sovereignty of self and self-guiding authority...A phenomenological ethics is not norm-oriented, nor does it flow from any authority, but constitutes itself as a phenomenology of lived ethics (Schirmacher, 1994).

Hanah Arendt puts forth that the concern with the self as the ultimate standard of moral conduct exists of course only in solitude. Its demonstrable validity is found in the general formula "It is better to suffer wrong than to do wrong," which, as we saw, rests on the insight that it is better to be at odds with the whole world than, being one, to be at odds with myself. This validity can therefore be maintained only for man insofar as he is a thinking being, needing himself for company for the sake of the thought process[8].

Isolation, on the other hand:

> ...occurs when I am neither together with myself nor in the company of others but concerned with things in the world. Isolation can be the natural condition for all kinds of work where I am so concentrated on what I am doing that the presence of others, including myself, can only disturb me. Such work may be productive, the actual fabrication of some new object, but need not be so.... Isolation can also occur as a negative phenomenon." (Arendt, P. 99)

The thinking being, as Arendt so clearly elucidates in *Eichmann in Jerusalem*, is one that is capable of judgment. Solitude is also a consideration for Schopenhauer, of course, but part of their suggestion, in suturing these horizons together, is that a person capable of judgment and 'moral' behavior, acts the same way in private as they do in public, without fear of the consequences. So it should be in the cyber-realm. Invoking Jean Francois Lyotard, Wolfgang Schirmacher asserts that "the ability of a self is not interested in the status quo of the databases, but is attracted to the sublime" (Schirmacher, 1994).

And it is in this that Heidegger's *Dasein* and more importantly his concept of the *Mitsein* comes into play. "Mitsein belongs to the being of Dasein that is an issue for its very being" (Schirmacher, 1994). Being-with, being in communion with, in community with, is at the very essence of what it means to be. We are active, engaged

---

8   It should be noted that both Judith Butler and Avital Ronell crystallized Arendt's thoughts in this passage, through their lectures "Have I been Destroyed (Ronell)," and "(Butler)". Youtube.com/egsvideo

(and engaging) dynamic beings and it is only in activity that we can truly be.

Then in locating the self, the sovereign in the cyber-realm is one that is open, self-generating, and being without any pre-given prescription of *demarcations* of identity, only the actuality of identity. The cyber-netizen, as sovereign, generates and exists in the cyber-realm. In discussing his concept of Homo-generator, Wolfgang Schirmacher states that the

> Homo generator anthropomorphically generates worlds without the need for any transcendental purpose outside of life itself. Such a life can make no claim for authenticity beyond itself, and in this sense it is artificial. 'An artificial life is led as the art of life, by a person who exists authentically, whose ethic is anthropologically characterized by openness (Schirmacher, 1994).

It means not allowing any division of our life, but creating and sharing in openness, not having to fear data which someone could gather on us, to bear in mind only that 'inter-subjective jobs can be public.' With that, it's not about being "forced to live publically", or answer "any question when asked", etc. The problem, as Schirmacher states, is not with privacy on the computer, but those whose "authoritarian power we have to fear" (Schirmacher 1994). Some of this has its traces in our fear of, and negotiation with, early authority figures. Authority, for the parent, is a means of not only exerting will, but to the thinking parent, capable of judgment (Arendt), it is a form of ethical training. Ethics exist as unstable coordinates, though, and behavior toward each other does not need the cyber-realm, or any techno-sphere, to act as a landscape-mediator. Ethical paradigms exist, but the implementation, the practice, seems to not largely be followed, and exist predicated upon subjectivity and situation (Nietzsche).

> Even a superficial analysis shows that the breakneck pace of the net-
> world's development is due above all to the fact than it offers simu-
> lated, user-friendly versions of useful, real-world institutions and
> services. Admittedly, the unpleasant sides of reality are increasingly
> catching up with this duplication of existing institutions, whether in
> the form of annoying network congestion or the large-scale appear-
> ance of con artists and militant right-wing radicals in the internet
> (Schirmacher, 1994)

Attempts to put issues of private and public space in the cyber-realm
still remain a conundrum. Companies like ReputationDefender
offer a promising short-term solution for those who can afford
it. With that said, basic tweaks for the online profile may not be
enough, as Web 3.0 is visible on the horizon. "A world in which
user-generated content is combined with a new layer of data ag-
gregation and analysis of live video" (Rosen, July 19 2010).

Rosen mentions the Facebook application, Photo Finder,
which uses facial recognition software (though quite tellingly,
early test runs of this application constantly miss faces whose ethnicity are not immediately recognizable, taking the notion of faciality in Facebook to another level).

At the moment, Photo Finder allows you to identify only
people on your contact list, but as facial-recognition technology
becomes more widespread and sophisticated, it will almost certainly challenge our expectation of anonymity in public. People
will be able to snap a cell phone picture (or video) of a stranger,
plug the images into Google and pull up all tagged and untagged
photos of that person that exist on the Web (Rosen, July 19, 2010).

In this configuration, Nakamura's cynicism is entirely
understandable—she has accepted vague arguments about
possibility as being the reality of the space, without recognizing that identities exist as such, from one space to another.

Moving Beyond Models and the Truth of Self

In his consideration of artificial life, Wolfgang Schirmacher provides a conceptual framework for living outside of trusted guidelines:

> Nowhere is this as evident as in the complete and irreversible collapse of the authoritative power ethics. Whether it is grounded ontologically, on utilitarian principles, or on those of natural law, ethical behavior in practice follows personal convictions which can be neither predicted nor effectively influenced. (Schirmacher, 1994)

A fluid ethical paradigm—we are not two blank slates sitting across from one another at the table. You bring your identities and your subjectivity, the limits of your horizon, just as I bring mine. Together, in our negotiation, in order for the ethical paradigm to have meaning or be effectively employed, it must either be a paradigm that we are both aware of—for ignorance of the paradigm will make it a pointless and one-sided exercise, or the paradigm must be fluid to allow for unforeseen flurries of emotion, unforeseen cultural misinterpretations or falsely construed insults, or even the diminishment of intended insults. Without the elasticity and the adaptability of any understanding of an ethical encounter, the encounter will surely fail.

Not that all communication is simply Source/ Message/ Encoder/ Decoder/ Receiver/ FeedBack/ Noise/, etc, or that the discussion of paradigms to imply strings and controls for encounters, but only the ecstasy of communication. Communication viewed through some precinct of ontology becomes a far more worthy, honest, and ethical endeavor—pushing past this nihilism of reductive models. If the coding and decoding of messages was all there was to it, we would live in a rather binary and largely uninteresting world.

While current media theory proposes that electronic media itself has become the 'message' and that its forms are to be understood as 'the extensions of man,' there still needs to be a fundamental shift in the understanding of media communication if not all information technology, and the theories that populate the discourse in order to truly embrace the cyber realm, and the self as part and parcel of it.

Interestingly enough the latest advancements in physical science indicate the primacy of form over function. Function is something that comes of form (whereas the reverse was thought to be the case for many years). This is something to note, as many years of philosophy have come to conclusions that support a similar feeling. And also the primacy of form over function , although function may, of course, have some place in the discussion. Bauhaus thinker Walter Gropius' daughter, Ati, was interviewed for a PBS Documentary about a decade or so ago. She took part in a documentary produced about 'visual thinking.' The basic notion she argued , much like her father (a Bauhaus thinker), was that form must always inherently follow function. The difficulty though, with this idea, is that it streamlined aesthetics into a geometric equation, and left little room for air. ... it also resulted in some ugly, if functional, furniture.

The experience of truth here is   authentic. The "I", in this sense, becomes the generator and sovereign of the cyber-netizen's life, and this is made possible by the acknowledgement of "myself" in the roles of performative self as father, performative self as coworker, performative self as media-maker, performative self as whatever role the netizen would happen to reveal in a situation, outside of the in-itself of authority. This leads to the idea of truth, the goal of interpretation, as a personal truth, which may as well be the role of a sovereign.

Gadamer works on this in his *Truth and Method*, where we

must fuse horizons—and in doing so we confront our prejudices and indeed, overcome them; this is wholly intrinsic. Authentic truth and self are found to shine through tradition, tradition of content, of regime, of anything at all. It communes with life, can commune with the living, and indeed, being as such in the cyber-realm shows us that. Identity (as process, as packs in lines of flight, as being) shines through.

Virtual worlds, aesthetic spaces, and random, everyday discourses are all equally accessible to an ethics of fulfillment, in the performance of which human beings generate themselves (homo generator). (Schirmacher, 1994)

It is, in other words, something more akin to life and living. The self then exists as part of this multiplicity in Kurzweil's coming singularity. It is not homogeneous, since the singularity itself functions as a mosaic.

PART II Sovereignty in Singularity's Second Negation

Chapter Three: On The Politics of Death in the Cyber Realm

Loss and Faciality in the Cyber-Realm
The Cyber Bully: Trauma, Authority, and Responsibility
Being Toward Death

For Plato, all Authority is—or at least, ought to be—founded on Justice or Quity. All other forms of Authority are illegitimate. This means, practically not stable, not durable, transient, ephemeral, accidental. In reality, all power that does not rest on Justice rests not on an Authority in the proper sense of the term. It is maintained only through force (through "terror")

–Kojève, 1964, p.77

Ethical phenomena and their sphere in the present life-world are perceived. In the age of technology with its sphere of artificiality, certain phenomena strike us and show themselves tous as ethical by sparking controversies about right and wrong behavior.

–Schirmacher, 1994

Loss and Faciality in the Cyber-Realm

The passage through borders is negated in the cyber-realm, since it exists as a border-less space. The transition of boundaries, in this instance the boundary concealed in life, of being and non-being, can be crossed in the off-line world, but how does one maintain dominion or sovereignty over this passage, and what is left in the wake in the cyber-realm?

> What is it then to pass the terms of one's life (*terma tou biou*)? Is it possible? Who has ever done it and who can testify to it. The "I enter," crossing the threshold, this "I pass" (Derrida, 1993, P. 8).

The notion of passage is one that is problematic in its Aporia, as questions of permeability, accounting for and to, and the imbuing of otherness come into the fray. Who owns my death, who prescribes ownership, where is my sovereignty and authority in death? Empathy and ethics both continue in the face of dying and death, and the mourning rituals present in the off-line world, become adapted in the cyber-terrain. What is left behind? What are the politics of life, death, and other-ing in the cyber-realm where the image of the faced can live on in perpetuity?

Faciality, as understood by Deleuze and Guattari in *A Thousand Plateaus,* begins with European racism. According to Michael Hardt, when considering this notion, the white man's claim has never operated by exclusion, or by designation of someone as Other: it is instead in primitive societies that the stranger is grasped as an "other."

Racism (per their example) then operates by the determination of degrees of deviance in relation to the White-Man face. From the viewpoint of racism, there is no exterior, there are no people on the outside. There are only people who should be like us and whose crime it is not to be. The dividing line is not between inside and outside but rather is internal. Faciality, then, as processed in a non-dialectical sense, operates as the representation of the order of rule.

Very specific assemblages of power impose significance and subjectification as their determinate form of expression... no signification without a despotic assemblage, no subjectification without an authoritarian assemblage, and no mixture between the two without assemblages of power that act through signifiers and act upon souls and subjects. "...A concerted effort is made to do away with the body and corporeal coordinates....Bodies are disciplined, corporeality dismantled, becomings-animal hounded out.... A single substance of expression is produced." (Deleuze and Guattari, 1987, P. 180)

Considering expression in his work *Cinema 1*, Deleuze provides the terms 'perception image' and 'affection image,' in describing the view of the character, and then the close up. The first deals with perception of perception, remembering that the camera "remains subject to the condition" (Deleuze, 1986, P. 67). The affection image, on the other hand, is the close up as such. It is then the quality of a thing without reference to anything else. The expression is the entirety of the image. The two poles of the face, in Deleuze's understanding, revolves around *power* and *quality*. What quality do we see in the image of a face?

When a part of the body has had to sacrifice most of its motoricity in order to become the support for organs of reception, the principal feature of these will now only be tendencies to movement or micro-movements which are capable of entering into intensive series, for a single organ or from one organ to another. The moving body has lost its movement of extension, and movement has become movement of expression. It is this combination of a reflecting, immobile unity and of intensive expressive movements which constitutes this affect. But is this not the same as a Face itself? (Deleuze, 1986, P. 87)

Translating this view to the cyber-realm, a consideration of the number of faces we see on a given 'page' (i.e., Facebook), needs to be taken into consideration. When Facebook offers to 'connect to new friends,' an image is attached to the invitation. Generally, the image is that of a face. If all the other information is concealed, and the cyber-netizen does not experience instant recognition, all she is left with is the affect, resulting in a decision whether or not to reach out or retreat. Whether or not one chooses to connect, then, is entirely dependent upon faciality. This is the production of what is considered normal, what is allowed to be seen.

> The organization of the face is a strong one. We could say that the face holds... a whole set of traits, faciality traits, which it subsumes and places at the service of significance and subjectification. ...If the face is a politics, dismantling the face is also a politics involving real becomings, an entire becoming-clandestine. Dismantling the face is the same as breaking through the wall of the signifier and getting out of the black hole of subjectivity (Deleuze and Guattari, 1987, P. 188)

Deleuze and Guattari bring the line of flight concept into play, through both the dismantling sense, and the constituent sense. That is, a removing of identification markers to a freeing line of flight, and to compose lines of flight together in a way that one line does not overtake the other line. That one identity, in this case, does not negate another, or that there is no colonizer/colonized relationship. The possibility of this negation, though, is quite strong—

> There is no guarantee that in dismantling my face this will ensure co possibility with you; we must, in the project of love, find the lines

with which we make compositions...It can happen in love that one person's creative line is the other's imprisonment. The composition of the lines, of one line with another, is a problem, even of two lines of the same type. There is no assurance that two lines of flight will prove compatible, co possible. There is no assurance that a love, or a political approach, will withstand it (Deleuze and Guattari P. 205).

An antidote to this equation includes an openness for ethical encounters, and fidelity to the ethical encounter—bearing in mind that compassion reveals itself when it is not, in Schirmacher's terms, *occasional compassion.* (Schirmacher, 1985) That is, the momentary compassion one indulges in when giving a quarter to a homeless person on a side walk, or a seventy-cents-a-day compassion to a "distant neighbor" (Schirmacher, 1985). This moment is more closely connected to guilt, a guilt of superiority—that internal hierarchy placing self above all others, and a fabrication of pity. "Compassion as a way of living will (be) tangible for us only when it has been bent back into an active sensitization" (Schirmacher, 1985).

Zizek calls this *cultural capitalism* (Zizek, 2010). In other words, the kind of capitalism that on one hand procures vast amounts of wealth for Soros or for the Starbucks Corporation, while on the other hand giving some of the profit back to the community, or some of the profit to a political cause, and so on. In other words, "when you buy a cup of coffee (at Starbucks) you're buying a coffee ethics" (Zizek, 2010). The problem that remains is this: by this form of compassion, a temporary bandage may be used to conceal, and yet not heal, a larger problem. While it addresses surface concerns, such as, perhaps, fixing an unprivileged child's cleft-palette, it does nothing to solve the problem of the underprivileged that originated their poverty-stricken lifestyle in the first place

Active compassion, then, moves past the darker logic of faciality, and into affect, and then action in the ethical encounter.
This realization is not immediate, even when experiencing the immediacy of the cyber-realm.

In a recent *Newsweek* Article, columnist Lisa Miller continued
the conversation about "the uses and abuses of virtual grief."
(Miller, February, 2010). The highlighted text sang out, "Will the
pages of the dead outnumber the living (on Facebook)? Will our
children be content to memorialize us with a quip on a 'wall'?"
(Miller, P. 24, 2010)

This, in part, was a response to Facebook's altered policy in the
light of the Virginia Tech murders—a number of people wished
for their friends' pages to remain "active," in order to have some
sense of shared grief and communion for those who had been
killed. Facebook now allows pages to remain 'active' in perpetuity for those who have passed, unless a family member requests
the page be taken down. At first Miller gives a bit of a nuanced
response to this kind of 'virtual mourning,' by stating,
"Here is a real gathering place, where friends can grieve together-
and where the deceased continues in some sense to exist" (Miller,
2010).

This kind of rhetoric is not sustained throughout the article.
After all, this section of the magazine is simply titled, 'religion,' so
the quoted demagogues of institutionalized religion need to step
in and make the case that this virtual grief is not a substitution for
the process of grief and mourning, which must include church-
approved rituals of burial and proximity of remains to family.
Death, in this instance, no longer belongs to the cyber-netizen,
but to those affected by her death. But does death ever truly reside
with us? Can we have domain over our own passing? "Even my
Being Toward Death (Heidegger) is not my own," Avital Ronell
has said (Ronell, 2010).

In describing the event, Jean-Francois Lyotard postulated
that, "The event always depends on the individual: an occurrence

becomes an event because a feeling perceives it as an event. As long as computers are not permeable, they hinder the event for people" (Schirmacher and Lyotard). An event in cyber-space, such as death, is real—a person is affected by the loss. A real loss has ritual, now, in the cyber-realm.

The question of death is one in which that "singularity in its different guises proposes a philosophy that faces death, not as a topic of conversation of the object of dialectical sublation" (Peters, P. 211, 2004)

In the collection of essays *Making Sense of Dying and Death*, Gary Peters offers a thoughtful essay on temporality and singularity. In it, he argues that philosophy of singularity raise:

> ...the thought and the thinker above the horrific nullity of its visage—but as the limit of philosophy itself and the failure of its absolute ambition. In fear, trembling, and anxiety, the philosophy of singularity confronts the temporal continuity of philosophical systems, reaching its apotheosis in the absolute idealism of Hegel—with the racial discontinuity of a lived time that ends. And, what is more, a lived time that ends alone, in absolute solitude outside of reassuring philosophical discourses (Peters, 211).

Despite what one may argue about death and ownership, it is the state in which dasein ends.

The Cyber Bully

Trauma

Schopenhauer once stated, "Society is in this respect like a fire— the wise man warming himself at a proper distance from it; not coming too close, like the fool, who, on getting scorched, runs away and shivers in solitude, loud in his complaint that the fire burns" (Schopenhauer, 2008). Schopenhauer was making an argument for solitude, while arguing against hyper-fabricated dialogue in society—a kind of role playing posed as communication. In rejecting this model, Schopenhauer argued for the self existing outside of, as Adorno referred to it, the social web of delusion. One could imagine Schopenhauer's response to Megan Meier's passing.

Megan Meier, according to her parents, was a shy girl, slightly overweight, who not unlike many girls her age wished to fit in, but did not fit the fashionable mold. In the reports following her death, her father indicated Megan had issues with depression, self-deprecation, and an unfulfilled desire to be respected and appreciated. These conditions lasted throughout her childhood. Enter her myspace.com account, and a meeting with Josh Evans, a young man who immediately indicated romantic feelings for her. He romanced her in the cyber-realm, in very PG-rated terms, but then suddenly grew hostile after months of gaining her trust, and became a cyber-bully. He insisted that the world would be better without Megan, and shortly thereafter, Megan hanged herself.
On the surface, this is the transformation for the concept of bullying—it no longer needs to have roots in our physical world, but in the ether of the cyber-realm. A lover's betrayal is not unique to social networking; it has long been a condition of romance as witnessed in plays, songs, films, and theater. The story becomes a bit more unique to the cyber-realm as the investigation of Josh Evans unfolded.

The story later broke that there was no Josh Evans, but rather, an empty avatar. 'Josh Evans' was a character invented by Lori Drew, the mother of Megan's former friend, who wished to get retribution through this cyber encounter. According to the police report following Megan's death:

> ...in the months leading up to Meier's daughter's suicide, she insti-
> gated and monitored a Myspace account which was created for the
> sole purpose of communicating with Meier's daughter (Pokin, 2007).

Thereafter, Megan's parents separated, due in part, they claim,
to the stress. Megan's mother formed a foundation to discuss
bullying and cyber bullying and is currently touring elementary
schools.

On one hand, this could be read as a sincere effort to ration-
alize her daughter's death and give it meaning. On the other,
the girl's decision to end her own life, a confirmation of the Will
(Schopenhauer), provides us with a more callous explanation.

> There are too many genuine evils in the world to allow our increas-
> ing them by imaginary misfortunes, which bring real ones in their
> train and yet this is the precise effect of the superstition which thus
> proves itself at once stupid and malign. (Schopenhauer)

A quick look at this website, though, gives a sense of grandstanding
in the face of a tragedy. Perhaps it is too cold to question a griev-
ing mother's motives, but with the studio-style portfolio headshot,
and speaking tour bookings, it becomes a question of sincere sharing, or grief as public spectacle.

In looking at the faciality paradigm, we see her as the antithesis of Otherness—white woman, dressed impeccably, situated in
an airbrushed photo where even her eyes have been given a glint.
The woman in this photo is privileged. Rather than an image of
mourning (or even a face of jubilation—behaving in her daughter's stead to discuss an issue at the heart of her passing), it appears
to be more of an 'about the author' photo. This is perhaps prefer-
able to a photo of raw grief, of raw affect-as-image, but it creates an
image designed for public relations in substitution for mourning.
In part, the image situated in this context promises an authority

on the subject of cyber-bullying, as though connection to a victim immediately makes one an authority on the subject. This kind of image is a culmination of misunderstanding of the mechanics of authority, something that is all too common.

In addition, the image purports the trappings of *melancholia*. Sigmund Freud provides some context to questions of loss and grief, and much of this has immediate application in the cyber-realm. In his essay, *Mourning and Melancholia*, Freud indicates two separate reactions to despair and trauma. The first is *mourning*, where loss is accepted. The second is *melancholia*, where loss is not allowed (Freud, 1922). Here, Freud suggests that 'self-laceration' is a way of preserving the other in our bodies. We are angry at the lost and strike out at them, now housed in ourselves. This is the basis of Freud's idea of the superego. Freud's way out of this bind is to say that there is a rage against the lost object; and in order to disengage this formation we must forget and let go of that other.

In the cyber-realm, we have an immediate problem facing this notion. On the one hand, Megan's death, a real tragedy with a real consequence, occurred to a cyber-interaction with a maliciously-intentioned adult. As part of the response, her mother initiated her quest—the tours, the web site, the deals, and so forth. No part of this suggests the 'letting go,' or 'acceptance' of Megan's parting, and in some way her death has become ritualized through the mediated encounters—a cyber call to never let this happen again.

In her work, Judith Butler discussed what happens if we think of Freud's melancholia as a cultural strategy? At a cultural level, where there are those that can't be mourned, we get a culturally-induced melancholia such that we don't have the vocabulary to describe the loss we have. The cyber-realm, then, can act against this form of cultural strategy. The mourning in the cyber-realm, through Facebook remembrances, and through cyber-netizen interactions, is a method of remembrance through mourning, and at the same time melancholia.

What keeps the melancholia alive is the *trauma* as suggested by Freud. Trauma, according to this paradigm, is what structures an identity. The truth was once affiliated with ruin and the resolution of the traumatic. Indeed, Laura Mulvey, in her iteration of Lacan suggests that identity formation begins with rejection. An infant catches her reflection, and immediately rejects the image before her. The conclusion is that we are more responsible for an untraceable cause than ever before with minimal signage and modest "moral devices" (Butler).

The connection then, is this: in order for true mourning to take place, the loss must be accepted, and there must be a moving on. Trauma remains, but trauma having been an agent of identity, it will continue to shape us even after moving on. Without this, we are locked into melancholia, in a space where true compassion can not exist.

Authority

Megan's action, which has triggered much of the conversation revolving around identity and ethics and cyber-bullying, was initiated by a tragic misunderstanding of her own self as authority. In his work *Notions of Authority*, Alexandre Kojève insists that authority is not about force, or "of forceable assertion itself as well," (Ronell, 2010) suggesting that it supersedes force with a "sovereign aloofness (Ronell, 2010)." But, according to Avital Ronell, Kojève misses that violence of *Language* (Lacan and later Zizek). This violence occurs in its most terrible form when the sovereignty of self is absent. The phenomenon of bullying stems from the abuse of power, whether physical, ideological, or systemic. It raises the question of the use of this kind of power, or the proper use of it. Does it always occur in times of systemic rule, or does this simply occur as part of human nature—the desire to be the alpha, and the desire to see others as subservient? It is not to say that the violence itself is not real, but it is to say that one can deflect the violence in the cyber-realm with the engaged inner authority, or at the very least, the "inner fuck you" (Sandy Stone).

In her paper, "Have I Been Destroyed Answering to the Question of Authority and the Politics of the Father," (presented in Saas-Fee, Switzerland), Ronell first addresses Hannah Arendt:

> These archaic sovereignties no matter how much we think we shed or molted them nonetheless still continue to send out by remote control or in your faces central command. (Ronell, 2009)

This could be either liturgical authority as commanded by the role of religion in the west (Giorgio Agamben), or in the role of authority in liberal capitalism and Zionism ever defended by our media and hierarchal structures (Zizek). Koejeve and Arendt also turn toward the vacant lot of divine abandonment where humankind is left to fend for itself in the "draught of monotheistic withdrawal. The Gods have fled...somehow authority is something that comes in as an emergency supply to fill up what is no longer there (Ronell 2009)."

In today's world, "...authority is being called back to conditions that can no longer hold authority together" (Ronell, 2009). In discussing the authoritative figure, and the performativity of authority, Ronell invokes a number of images from father, enemy, sovereign forces and legal forces, while also maintaining a critical eye toward the technocratic deterministic forces of institutionalized education, replete with its authoritative mandates.

Here, she argues, the self becomes destroyed under these forces, no longer capable of reaching out to gods in our post-metaphysical understanding, but to each other—although each one of us has had these kinds of forces pressed against us, and among many other means, violence and judgment.

The conundrum of judgment, though, is pared with responsibility and action. Hannah Arendt speaks about judgment throughout her work, including her seminal *Eichmann in Jerusalum*, (Arendt), where she, according to Judith Butler, enacts a judgment onto Eichmann in the book's closing pages. A question Butler raises is whether or not this act of judgment is one based in authority, or a performative authoritarian gesture.

Ronell continues, "propelled by the sense that all traditional forms of authority are collapsing, Arendt traces the destruction to the pre-political zones of education and child-rearing...where authority appears to be a natural" (Ronell, 2010). Ronell's objection is summed up in her parenthesis at the end of her presentation.

> As a toddler, I would have preferred more skill, some consideration, the occasional hug, and none of the poses of parental authority always completely off the mark, entirely unhelpful, and for all intents and purposes one big joke (Ronell, 2009).

This suggests that authority is linked with punishment, and that both are directly comprised under the notion of sovereignty. Let's take this a step further, then. Authority, judgment, punishment are all processes that are not directly biological-without-the-interference of biotechnical amplification of monitoring, and lie deep within the sovereignty of self. It can neither invade nor be invaded. Schirmacher ties this together nicely, stating that "this is the only authority I accept: the authority of skills, of thinking, of openness; an authority without punishment" (Ronell, 2010).

To Schirmacher, an authority is an authority that is understood in its own right. Schirmacher continues by identifying himself as sovereign, and this is the case that must be made again and again in discourses revolving around authority, punishment, and judgment.

To return to Megan's death—the desire to die overwhelmed the desire to live, and this connects into the non-exercise of her own authority through sovereignty-of-self. What becomes refutable is the notion that she needed to be given authority, though there is an inclination to believe her parents' actions, contrary to Arendt's direct plea that a child needs authority-through-rearing, and this actually created far larger damage in their interaction.

In sum, one of the great benefits of cyberspace--its power to act as an equalizer, tearing down pre-existing conceptions of societal gatekeepers--should not become its largest liability. Every idea may have equal legitimacy, but every action does not. The phenomenon of cyber-bullying will have no impact on those cyber-netizens who are engaged in their authority, through the sovereignty-of-self. Without this as a guiding force for a cyber-netizen, a fictitious character—an intentionally false identity created for (in this instance) malicious gains, therefore, should not act as a catalyst (not necessarily the cause) of a person's death. Identities in the cyber-realm can be as coarse as those encountered in our walking-world—where a total lack of empathy can exist, but does not require the shield of anonymity through fictitious avatars or internet handles—and such a lack of empathy in a person may simply exist constitutively and find further utility in the cyber-realm.

A sovereign cyber-netizen will find the right tools to navigate these annoyances—even by touching something as simple as an 'ignore,' or 'delete from friends' button. "Shrieking in the highest decibel" (Hughes) may now be sacramental for many who enter chat-rooms, social networking situations, or talkbacks in public forums. These voices, though, need to be regarded as voices encountered in one's walking life. The societal voices Schopenhauer urged us to keep distance from for fear of being burned or, in Deleuze and Guattari's terms, the voices that construct the destructive lines of flight.

Schopenhauer urges us to value silence. To value solitude,

not as a form of isolation-as-punishment or solitary confinement, but as a valuable way to spend time. Alone with one's thoughts. Finding peace within thoughts, while shutting out the 'blockheads' that can alter our self-esteem. This is not to say 'hell is other people,' as Sartre famously suggests in *No Exit*. Rather, don't let other people become your own hell. In channeling Schopenhauer's thoughts on death, Schirmacher offers: "death is conquered, as Schopenhauer would have it, when one discovers the worthlessness of life" (Schirmacher, 1994).

Responsibility

Who is ultimately responsible for Megan's death? The sovereign model immediately tells us that it is Megan, and Megan alone, and yet there is still a cry for compassion even within this paradigm. And there is a cry for justice for what the "Joshua Evans" avatar handlers have done—the situation they exacerbated in dealing with an apparently fragile thirteen-year-old child. There has been some suggestion through talkbacks that this was a form of manslaughter, or murder that had been committed in the cyber-realm. This claim becomes immediately refutable, as one must look at this event both legally and philosophically.

Legally, there was no intent to murder, at least none that can be proved beyond the shadow of a doubt. And if that legal motive does not exist, then the philosophical question becomes immediately clear, as Schirmacher defines the murderer's mindset: "the murderer mindset that places its own welfare thoughtlessly over all else and is not willing to deny itself any means, is masking itself as humanity" (Schirmacher, 1994).

This was a human interaction in cyber-space, and there *was* a disastrous consequence, but at no point could this be construed as murder. The motive, admittedly, was surely not a positive one—

there is never a good reason for an adult to harass a child, one must simply live by a higher standard, if age is to equate worldview.

Arendt has written extensively about responsibility in her work, in particular when discussing Adolf Eichmann, and of personal responsibility. (Arendt, 1995).   Arendt's "banality of evil" should be read as a clarion call: Eichmann is no different from any of us if we are not mindful of our supreme moral obligation to one another. Eichmann justified his behavior based on a reading of Kant and a belief that maintaining the order demanded by the State was the same thing as being moral. Hannah Arendt's *Eichmann in Jerusalem - The Banality of Evil* is a character study of the fissures present in our modern understanding of how politics is possible.

Her final judgment of Eichmann is that he is guilty because he acted in concert with people that believed that they had the ability to choose who was allowed to live on this earth and who was not. Her critique of the trial itself is that it failed to enunciate an even bigger problem facing all of humanity (and not just Israel): our laws are no longer able to comprehend the evil committed by the Nazis. Our laws are predicated on the belief that criminal behavior is the result of criminal intent and that the criminal subject can know the difference. The failure to think is his crime.

The lesson, then, is to put value on self, finding the inner sanctuary to heal, but also finding comfort through identity in order to make connections to the outer world. Perhaps it could be 'finding the inner ethical authority.' Thinking, a normative form of judgment, was not exercised in this case, but Joshua Evans (as avatar, or as the person behind the avatar) is hardly Adolf Eichmann— she probably is more in line with the caricature that Schopenhauer puts forth as the annoyingly common and antagonistic blockhead.

Being Toward Death

In these two examples, a reading of death, the remaining image, and mourning against melancholia have come into play. Being, vis-à-vis Heidegger, expresses the human experience in temporality—but this temporality is a method of order—that we actually exist in ecstasy. The order we attempt, as expressed by Deleuze and Guattari, is a line of flight in action and creation. This flight, then, transforms the compositions of order into components of passage—poros in the Aporia of *transformativity*. The structure of temporality, the organization of words in the description of perceived time passages, is, in part that order-word.

> For the question was not how to elude the order-word but how to elude the death sentence it envelops, how to develop its power of escape, how to prevent escape from veering into the imaginary or falling into a black hole, how to maintain or draw out the revolutionary potentiality of the order-word. (Deleuze and Guattari, 1987, P. 110).

The transformation as it resonates in the cyber-realm is one that exists beyond the being toward death, the absolute stalling of *dasein*—in perpetuity, or at least as long as the mainframes exist.

Identities remain after the body in the waking world has met its end, but the remembrances of the multiplicities are revealed in additional interactions in the cyber-realm. For instance, Jose Ramirez, a student from the State University of New York at New Paltz, passed away in January 2009. Immediately, a flood of sympathizers left messages and posts on Jose's Facebook wall. The latest message, as of this writing, occurred yesterday, when a friend posted a simple message, "thinking of you" over two years after his passing. This new virtual acceptance, if one were to evoke the five stages of grief, does more than accept loss—it keeps the memory of life, the archive alive even in the face of *being toward death*. "Death, then, is the own-most potentiality-for-being, non-relational, and not to be out-stripped" (Heidegger, 1962, P. 308). Heidegger used the terms "authentic," and "inauthentic," in describing two possibilities within Being For Death, against dasein. When by anticipation, one becomes free *for* one's own death, one is liberated from one's lostness in those possibilities which may accidentally thrust themselves upon one; and one is liberated in such a way that for the first time one can authentically understand the factical possibilities lying ahead of that possibility which is not to be outstripped. (Heidegger, 1962, P. 308)

In this configuration, then, the death is not an empirical death. An end, and as Derrida would have it, a translocation through a poros. If man creates self out of self, as homo generator or autopoiesis suggests, then man creates an end out of the ending. "In a culture of death, such as it needs an artificial life, even one's own death is self-engendered, a deed for which I am responsible" (Schirmacher 1994). Ultimately, it was Megan's failure to recognize her own sovereignty, even in an encounter devoid of ethics that lead to her death. Ultimately, death rituals in the cyber-realm give credence to Derrida's central question in *Aporias*. Being-for-death, the condition in which dasein is not a consideration, is one that is the final modality of self, beyond the mourning texts on Facebook walls.

Chapter Four: On Journalism Ethics in the Cyber-Realm

The Media Takeover
Singularity and New Media
Faciality and the Mosque Shooting
The Current Model
Satire as a Means of Bearing Witness

> *Habermas offers us an ethics of modernity: in the transformation of inter-subjective convictions into a social force through the participation of an informed public.*

–Wolfgang Schirmacher

> *When the press is free, and every man able to read, all is safe.*

—Thomas Jefferson

The Media Takeover

In his *Introduction* to *Homo Generator: Media and Post Modern Technology*, Wolfgang Schirmacher asks "what is *real?*" A more specific question might be, what is *real* in media? Where can we find *authentic truth* in representation, not in the agreed constructed actualities? In media discourses, we are told by large networks that they operate beyond biases, that what you have is not subjectivity, but the pursuit of objectivity and fairness. Balance of ideas that move beyond a simple *disjunctive synthesis* (Deleuze) and present notions in opposition, argued with the fullness of rhetoric.

These claims, however, do not stand up to any basic test. Habermas may have offered the "inter-subjective convictions into a social force through the participation of an informed public," but if that public is misinformed, barely-informed, or not at all informed either through willful ignorance or the collapse of the fourth estate, the public can not authentically participate.

Schirmacher puts it succinctly: "Today, the media have largely taken over the role of the authorities who are never at a loss for an answer" (Schirmacher, 2004). In this text, he was evoking Paul Virilio to a degree, but he also shares this view in additional writings when talking about the media artist, or even the journalist. What is the role of the journalist?

In a recent lecture given at the State University of New York, New York Times columnist and journalist Dan Barry described his job as "bearing witness." Barry has been a part of *The New York Times* since 1995, has written columns under several meta-headings during that time, and has earned a number of awards including the Pulitzer Prize and the George Polk Award. With these credentials seasoning his biography, he broke down his journalistic trade to 'bearing witness.'

At the same time Barry, a veteran of the newspaper industry, addressed the multi-media storytelling in its practices, but maintained the theme of bearing witness, and spoke of it as a subjective experience.

"Someone is paying me to go to where you're not going to tell you what it looks like, feels like, smells like and sounds like" (Brandi, 2010). Yet, it looks as though we can know only what we ourselves discovered as witnesses to a truth lived personally. "We are victims and victimizers of life and, therefore, maybe not the most trustworthy witnesses (ask animals and plants about it), but I am the only me I've got" (Schirmacher, 1994).

In part, Barry is correct. The job that he, and many other professionals take on well, is that of one who bears witness, and brings findings to the public. But Barry may be a dying breed—conceptual truth may be difficult to locate. "Truth is a gift of *dasein*" (Schirmacher, 1994) and to represent this truth is a task that the larger media structures, such as Fox News, MSNBC, and CNN have put aside in favor of the bottom line—after all, media is a business, which means it must serve the investors and advertisers if it is to survive.

In the representation of reality, Schirmacher offers the terms *virtual* and *artificial*. Schirmacher insists that the term *virtual* as in *virtual reality* is an approximation of reality, an almost-reality, while the term *artificial* has been greatly reduced to mean *fake*-a concept he fights against. He sets up these terms to move us into a new understanding of *artificial life*, that is life that is lived artfully, and human as, in part, artifice of nature and the universe. For artificial life, then, acts as real life, and human beings act as self generators in autopoiesis.

In understanding news media in these terms, humans who make story material through interfaces such as the news reel of long ago, the television set, and now through the cyber-realm have an awesome responsibility—to represent our lives in artificial life, to push us to live bodily in all arenas of life, and to foster ethical encounters in intercultural communication.

The failing, then, cannot be underestimated. In looking at artifice and technology, Schirmacher asks "Does the simulation of creativity in communication technology challenge a negative dialectics of technology: death technologies versus life technologies, being mediocre versus becoming oneself, participating versus originating?" (Schirmacher, 1994)

Traditional models of media have suffered under the onslaught of corporate control. Corporations (and therefore the corporatization of media) are not the disease, but rather a symptom of a system whose only purpose is to self-perpetuate and grow on a profit model. There is a meta-structure above the corporation, and media has become a casualty of it.

Wolfgang Schirmacher, Neil Postman, Paul Virilio and others have employed the term Homo Faber, that is of humans behaving as technological and tool innovators. Here, Schirmacher makes a distinction in introducing Homo Generator "the media artist as generator of human reality and his or her responsibility for tomorrow's artificial world" (Schirmacher, 1994).

Where can one find the homo generator in action? Where is the responsibility in the new media terrain? Who is the media artist as generator of human reality?

Singularity and New Media

In consideration of the singularity, in this case the element of the singularity which purports the growth of information technology—which can move faster than formulations of laws or even of ethical paradigms questions of who can bear witness arises. The location of professional ethics in journalism is less static than in the traditional newsroom, when there is time to edit a story, and even give the occasional call of 'stop the presses.' What if there are no presses to stop just the ebb and flow of information as a signal? When journalist Kevin Sites left his job at a large media company (NBC), he ventured into a new foray: an online news magazine and documentary format. Sponsored by Yahoo!, the Kevin Sites *In the Hot Zone* website followed the *Daniel Pearl Award* winning journalist through twenty-two spots of 'conflict' around the globe. Part of his mission was to remove his reporting from the influence of the corporate news filters, and show original images of conflict without sanitization. According to a recent television interview in the Hudson Valley, New York, Sites saw this as an escape from the media structure. He argued that he was pushing back against questions of so called "non-filtered stories," presented as 'original' pieces. The mission lasted a year, and then the site was promptly taken down—the video pieces were all merged in the creation of a longer form documentary with a narration by Sites.

As for what the site had been: at the first glance of Kevin Sites' website, we are greeted with an orange banner (a Yahoo! News Banner), with a silhouetted (presumably Sites) figure, holding a small video camera, sporting a back pack. We see several images (links) that will direct us to different sections of his documentary (a retrospective of his experiences), and are greeted with a clean, photo-manipulated head shot of Sites, beside a link to what he calls his 'mission statement.' Some links will take us to photo-essays, other links will take us to videos and video blogs, while other links will take us to site-user talk backs. While this blending of mediated forms is immediately attractive, it calls several large questions and ideas into play.

In recognizing the inter-connection of media related to re-search, reading, articulation, ontology, and epistemological approaches does give shape to criticism aimed at Kevin Sites.

First, there is no 'original' in media any longer, with regard to the medium as tactile artifact. Who can call a video posted on Kevin Sites in the Hot Zone an original? Already, the video is an electronic reproduction of a signal—the visual and audio signals given off by what is in front of a camera. From there, through the steps of electronic manipulation (editing), and selection of the story, followed by posting on an internationally accessible platform, we have a story that is filtered-perhaps not by corporate influence, but by relativist human decision making. There are no 'original' photographs either. A photographic file can be exported at the same resolution to any number of computers, or uploaded to any server, and sent out on the World Wide Web. Any printed image of the photograph or any virtual rendering from machine to machine is already a copy without an original. With these converged forms of media, it is simultaneously liberation of meaning from the broadcast structure, but also a hindrance to meaning as all the forms become de-contextualized.

Jean Baudrillard calls the phenomenon of a copy without an original *simulacrum*. Baudrillard offers a number of essays in his book, *Simulacra and Simulation*, among them, "Implosion of Meaning in the Media" (Baudrillard, 1994 P. 79). In this essay, Baudrillard hypothesizes three possible correlations between media and meaning, and ultimately rationalizes the three with a significant statement: "where we think information produces meaning, the opposite occurs." Baudrillard continues his criticism, suggesting that the media "exhausts itself in the act of staging communication," and "the media are not the producers of socialization, but of exactly the opposite, of the implosion in the social in the masses" (Baudrillard, 1994, Pp. 80-81). The text concerns pirate media, and forms of anti-media, which he suggests are also slaves to the medium and therefore tantamount to the hiding of the real in even non-traditional media.

Kevin Sites' goals, including the disruption of the hard structured media-corporations, is already subservient to a mechanism that devours any stab outside of the mechanism (such as the cultural industry), into the very mechanism he is attempting to escape. For example, while lashing out at corporate media, Sites has agreed to sponsorship by Yahoo!, which is simply another corporation. The profit model is a bit different, and therefore there is arguably more room for Sites to render controversial material, but it is still part of the corporate process. Baudrillard's concerns for 'pirate media' and 'anti-media' are well-founded.

In addition to these concerns of original verses produced, there is the concern about openness, the aporetic openings in the encounter. As Schirmacher states, "Openness is the last thing the representatives of the status quo want to permit in the net" (Schirmacher, 1994). Looking at the cross-pollination of mediated forms, we see these forms existing in *liminal* spaces. A working definition of the *liminal* would be a conscious state of being on or between two existential planes; indeterminacy or sense of identity dissolves a bit as normal limits are relaxed. These spaces do call for openness of interaction. Both structure and anti-structure are possible. The normal limits of broadcast censorship are removed. The normal limits of viewing media via a tube, unabated with the aid of a mouse or keyboard, are no longer in play. There is no hard time, or hard broadcast cycle, for the content to appear. The media is now interactive, as the user is able to make decisions about what item to 'click,' or if the user wishes to make a 'post' for talk-back of course the talk-back is an illusion of talk-back, as Haraway herself has suggested there is no substitute for face to face encounters— spoken or textual language is one of many languages human beings use when interacting (Haraway, 2003).

Another question to consider revolves around Sites, himself. Who is he? Is Sites, showcased at the center of this website ultimately more important than the stories he's bringing to the surface? Also, why select *these* stories? Is he proposing solutions, or is this merely a form of pornographic journalism and virtual poverty tourism? In considering Sites' role, Walter Benjamin comes into the foray. Benjamin has posited that the artist is inconsequential when compared to the work itself. In broad terms, he is talking about the importance of the existence of the artifact, and the experience of the artifact (or aura created in the experience of the artifact) having greater weight than the hands that rendered it.

In fairness, this is a bit of an oversimplification, but at its core this is a part of Benjamin's presentation. Can the same be said when looking at specific areas of media? Is the reporter inconsequential to the story? Or is a story inconsequential to the company whose logo begins the story (NBC, Yahoo, etc)? If taken a step further, can we assume that all media is then created in a vacuum? Or is the reductive de-contextualizing of the anthropologic and business factors a danger to a better understanding? Perhaps the more valid stance is that they are all part of the form, all part of the primacy of form, and therefore the form (which includes the above considerations in the form's batter) becomes a wholeness of these variables.

Of course, Benjamin does not necessarily see the politicizing of art (and by extension, media) as a negative. He suggests that art can be political, but there are various uses in art; politics of resistance and mass distraction to name two (Benjamin, 2008, P. 56). Perhaps Sites has offered something reactionary to the politicizing of media, and the mass distraction concept, while attempting to not fall victim to the notion of culture industry co modification, and has done so by fusing media forms (liminal space) into a new meta-form. This could be the answer to Baudrillard's concerns over 'pirate media,' or 'anti-media,' except that he still has Yahoo! as sponsor. After all, is rebellious anti-authority music truly against invisible authority structures when brought to us by Pepsi? How rebellious can Eminem claim to be when shilling IPods? Is anti-corporate media truly anti-corporate if brought to us by Yahoo!?

Faciality and The Mosque Shooting

We are back to the vicious cycle of terror breeding terror, from both ends of the political spectrum. With both the government and the non-state group claiming that, they are victims of horrific terror and violence imposed by the other. The argument about which victim is more worthy of pity and vengeance is truly vulgar, it is nothing more than a vulgar "ethical illusion" (Abdunnur, 2010, p. 135).

As mentioned earlier, Deleuze and Guattari offer the concept of faciality. Levinas' notion of the Face of the Other is expanded here, "The face is not an envelope exterior to the person who speaks, thinks, or feels " (Deleuze and Guattari, 1987, P. 167). In their dialogue, which includes what they call *significance* and *subjectification*, they contend that the system reverts to a white wall/black hole system. "The colonist constructs the dark other and attributes to it racial quality...negating this colonialist forms in its own identity" (Deleuze and Guattari, 1987, P. 167).

In this instance, Kevin Sites acts as 'the white colonist,' against a backdrop of 'dark other.'

> If the face is a politics, dismantling the face is also a politics involving real becomings, an entire becoming-clandestine. Dismantling the face is the same as breaking through the wall of the signifier and getting out of the black hole of subjectivity (Deleuze and Guattari, 1987, P. 188).

Kevin Sites appears in the video, and on the computer screen, as a young, white, athletic "non-threatening" male—clearly descendant of Europeans. As such, he travels into either Eastern-European or non-white countries, such as Iraq and Lebanon, to offer a world-news view of conditions in the spots of conflict. As the face and voice of the conflict, he is self-assured, and also mysteriously out of place in the picture. In a sense, he has become and ethnographic documentary filmmaker. He is not, in any way, shape or form a representative of the region in which he reports, he is not part of the cultural scenery, and instead operates as the outsider and our insider. This immediately negates trustworthiness to his presence, as the gains seem to be for his reputation, and not necessarily the story of place.

Faciality does not operate by "exclusion" or by "designation," and racism operates by the "determination of degrees of deviance to the White Man's face." (Deleuze and Guattari, 1987, P. 188) Faciality then, propagates "waves of sameness." Those who resist this form of identification will be wiped out, as will those who "allow themselves to be identified by a "degree of divergence." Deleuze and Guattari continue on by saying that its "cruelty is equaled only by its incompetence and naïveté."

In November 2004, as an NBC correspondent, Sites videorecorded an incident involving a US soldier. Sites was embedded with a group that had overtaken an Iraqi militant faction in a mosque. The US soldiers made make-shift beds and make-shift accommodations for their wounded prisoners of war. Shortly after, gunshots were heard in the streets, and US soldiers, along with Sites, exited the mosque. While outside, another group of US soldiers entered the mosque, and began executing the prisoners of war. In fact, Sites captured a video image of one US soldier pointing to an unarmed wounded Iraqi in the mosque, stating, "look at him. He's pretending to be fucking dead," before killing the unarmed man on camera (Sites).

The murderer/soldier was an American, though the video quality was such that his features were immediately difficult to place—his voice, mannerisms, and uniform all indicate service to the United States. The murdered man did not have an aesthetic connectable to the European features—dark skin, dark hair, and his confederates (also murdered save for one) look regional Arabic—other in the eyes of the American troops.

On the *Hot Zone* site, Sites has a confessional style video, describing his thoughts when sending the video back to NBC. When Sites sent this report back to NBC, he edited out the execution, believing that his job was to 'minimize harm.' Sites felt that if the entire section had been aired, or if the footage were seen by opposition forces, nobody would have surrendered to the US, believing they would be executed upon the moment of surrender. A stern warning can be found in *A Thousand Plateaus*: "First we must recognize our place in hierarchy, but in dismantling this we must ensure we don't lose our Face (lest we end up in a gas chamber)" (Deleuze and Guattari, 1987, P.188).

The murdered man was slain under the identifiers that differentiate him from the American soldiers: simultaneously, Kevin Sites acts as a buffer between western-viewer and events on the screen due to his white Anglo appearance.

> This machine is called the faciality machine because it is the social production of the face, because it performs the facialization of the entire body and all its surroundings and objects, and the landscapification of all worlds and milieus (Deleuze and Guattari, 1987, P. 181).

Sites claims he later second-guessed this decision, and feels he had mislead the public by not showing an accurate portrait of war, and for allowing his content to be filtered. In his own words, he felt 'complicit' in being part of the filter machinery. This led to his decision to leave NBC and join Yahoo! as a solo journalist.

Taking Sites' motives as genuine, it is clear he desired to seek out an alternative vessel for his journalistic leanings. The ethical question looms, and continues to loom, with regard to rules of journalistic engagement, integrity, and responsibility in war. NBC did hide the truth: they disguised it in order to not put the public on alert, or alert enemies, but then when the truth is so obscured, regardless of rationale, does this not bring the machinery itself into question? Are facts to be constantly hid from the masses with the flimsy rationale of protecting the masses? If eviscerated, or side stepped, or omitted for other reasons , then the entire apparatus becomes suspect. This applies to all media and mediums, regardless of form.

The Current Model

According to their web site,

> Current Media is an award-winning multiplatform company dedicated to the in-depth investigation and exploration of the world's most important, interesting, and entertaining stories. With a fully integrated broadcast and online platform, Current connects its audience with what's going on in their world through its unique blend of original productions and viewer created media (Current.com).

What the PR introduction does not immediately indicate is its process: it is created, almost exclusively, out of 'viewer created content.' Current was the brain-child of former United States Vice President Al Gore, and John Hyatt, who acts as its CEO. The company was formed in 2002, and has already earned an Emmy-- the youngest television network ever to do so. The viewer-created paradigm has shifted over time. Initially, the cable network co-incided with its web site. That is, a media creator would upload a video-pod to the web site; that pod would receive a certain number of votes; and the pods that had the most votes (by other users) would be aired on the national network.

The model proved to be less-than-sustainable, and so it shifted, in part, to include a more traditional newsroom in San Francisco, linkages with rottentomatoes.com for merged entertainment content, and other original programming. It still allows users to upload videos, and some do wind up on the air, but that model is no longer primary.

In expanding its uses, site users now will be able to chat, add to feedback, and also contribute through texts and webcam uploads, and link other sites to the story in the feedback. It is multi-platform, while also retaining the cable network.

Research by the network indicates that 70% of its viewers have their laptop open as they watch Current TV on cable. The new site will allow those viewers to interact immediately with content, voting for top stories, which will rise to the top of the home page. (Haughstead, 2007)

Market research aside, the site operates best when fully engaged with a variety of media around it—pulling reports from the *New York Times*, the Huffington Post, Viewer Created Content, as well as original vanguard programming. What makes this model particularly effective is the inter-activity among users, and this may serve as a future model for blogosphere and backpack journalists looking to glean professional credentials. Interactivity is key. Perspective is subtractive, akin to holding a flashlight in an otherwise dark room.   It is possible, in this image, to move the light around the room, in an attempt to piece the larger picture together from memory, and then operate from that memory as if all has been revealed. Such is the analogy for large corporate media, their flashlight corresponding to that of the dollar bill, —even taking the faciality paradigm into account.

Perception, however, can be additive. Gadamer spoke about bringing horizons together in *Truth and Method*, and in admitting biases the first step to shared perception comes into focus. With multiple perspectives, such as current.com allows, it is possible for the cyber-netizen to engage in ethical encounters—producing, consuming, creating, speaking, sharing. Multiple flashlights added into the room reveal a larger picture.

This perhaps utopian idea still falls short, though. The talk-backs in this section (a sampling of seven random news stories) demonstrates a small number of talk-backers who argue over the same round of semantics. The words 'liberal' as a slur and 'conservative' as an insult are the most often used terms. With a space of such possibility, how can one move past this to truly bear witness? While journalism ethics and paradigms exist, they do not exist outside of our broader understanding of ethical encounters, or of sovereignty for the cyber-netizen for that matter. While the negotiations about these non-fixed points continue, we will still continue to grapple on who we surrender our own ability to bear witness to.

Or better yet, we will embrace Homo Generator, and Homo Faber, and recognize that media creation through technology is something everyone is capable of. This will not only level the playing field, but fuse populations of horizons in creating our new media and journalism understanding.

In today's world a communicative aesthetics tells us that our perception is always mediated and that all forms of mediation are equally important. How we perceive our world is shaped by the media in such a fundamental way that perception and media become interchangeable. Such an observation is bound to be misunderstood as long as media is defined as a sender for which we are the receiver.

Aesthetics and aesthetic experience then drive the conversation when negotiating the terrain, separating the viewer from those who would bear witness for us. The aesthetics give us a sense of urgency—the graphic elements, the quick interfacing and interloping of information and non-information alike. In reading the aesthetics that drive the news media, a voice outside of the con-

figuration is needed in order to bear witness to the news outlet—
bearing witness to those who would bear witness.

Satire as a Means of Bearing Witness

In their paper, *Primacy Effects of 'The Daily Show' and National TV
News Viewing: Young Viewers, Political Gratifications, and Internal
Political Self-Efficacy* (Holbert, R.; Lambe, J; Dudo, A; and Carlton,
K. March 2007), the authors examine the 'political gratifications'
associated with viewing *The Daily Show.* They suggest that "The
Daily Show offers a satirical critique of various elements of U.S.
democracy, capitalism, and…journalism, as a profession." They
also add that *The Daily Show* offers a "radically different perspective" (Holbert, R.; Lambe, J; Dudo, A; and Carlton, K. March
2007),   as a source for political information. One could take it a
step further.

They conclude, "…but the broader message of this work is a
call for the discipline to not study entertainment and public affairs content in relative isolation" (Ibid). This may be appropriate
for the methodology the authors have outlined, but I would argue
for a study either of those who avoid satire and intake traditional
forms of media, next to those who take in alternative forms of
media, while not consuming traditional models. It would be in-
teresting to study their leanings, the kind of discourse they engage
in when discussing politics, or current events, and then to test the
results side by side.

The program may be replete with seemingly sophomoric pot-
shots, but it brings context to national events that most media
does not jump on. A question Holbert et. al ask is whether the
program acts in a manner that supplants regular news consumption for an audience, or if it is an ancillary program that helps cit-

izens better understand the news of the day. This question alone seems to accept that *The Daily Show* *is* affecting, and possibly shaping, the political views of at least part of the audience. Is the audience using *The Daily Show* as their only news source, or is it part of larger political media consumption?

News is not performing its task any longer. Satire has maintained relevancy. In a recent interview with MSNBC's Rachel Maddow, Jon Stewart defended his role as satirist, stating, "this box (satire) has always existed."

> The conflict we've bought into is left, right. Red, blue. The news networks bought into that...they have this idea that the fight in Washington is republican democrat. Why not isolate that and stand back here and let them go at it. And what it does is amplify a division that I don't think is the right fight...both sides have their way of shutting down the debate, and the news networks have allowed these two sides to become the fight...and I think the fight in the country is corruption verses non-corruption (Rachel Maddow interviews Jon Stewart).

The jester is the only member of the court who can poke fun at the king, while maintaining his head. As such the jester is given leeway to put out truth masked in humor in a way that others seem incapable of. Satire is liminality. It exists in the openings of being comedy, becoming comedy, becoming news, becoming information, a fusion of perception with subjective leanings in the Aporia. The show provides a counter point. That it does so in an entertaining fashion is a bonus, although it's not necessary. In fact, some of the better moments in the program are the quiet conversations with guests such as Richard Clarke, John McCain, and Colin Powell.

With Mr. Powell, Jon Stewart sought to understand how The United States was lead into Iraq, based partially on Powell's presentation from a few years earlier. Stewart mentioned that in grade school his math teacher instructed students to 'show their work'—so that the teachers may see how the student reached the mathematic conclusion. Jon Stewart asked Mr. Powell why the administration felt it did not need to 'show their work' to the public before concluding that the Iraq invasion was necessary.

Where does that leave us? Many issues have surfaced in a rough examination, even through preliminary questioning, of the role of converging media, and how this could affect truth, our culture industry, and simulated communication models. If media is obscuring truth and filtering its objectives with the desire to protect the military industrial complex, thoughts of patriotism, and larger corporate concerns, then it seems rather close to death. On the other hand, there is this fragile enterprise online, which could also fall victim to the culture industry. While large media outlets find a way to create their own venues in cyberspace, other varieties of alternative media (anti-media, and the new pirate media) arrive to challenge the larger structures out in the blogosphere, and other evolving venues in cyberspace. And now, Kevin Sites walks a fine line with how he's sponsored, and continues to sponsor, *his* enterprise.

Will we see truly converged synergy across mediated platforms? By all accounts, we have. It is the motive that remains in question, and not necessarily the technology itself. The cross-pollination of mediated forms existing in liminal spaces is especially important for a more thorough investigation. Perhaps there exists a 'fifth estate' within the hybrid form, which allows for both the advent of 'structure and anti-structure' to *strangely* co-exist. The question, precisely and invariably, rests upon the possibility of its existing *motive*.

As corporate news online and on television becomes more and more like Fox News (i.e., working as a shill for political machinery as opposed to providing information for a public to make political and social decisions), the question of who will bear witness remains.

In a recent conversation with Rachel Maddow, John Stewart asserts that the role of the satirist has always been present—from the court jester to those who would speak to truth about a variety of important issues through a comedic lens. In other words, when satire works at its optimum capacity, a viewer may find herself nodding emphatically in agreement—hearing a thought that she herself had attempted to articulate or contextualize, but was unable to. Satire provides the context for this kind of understanding. The satirist remains absolutely critical in bearing witness in order for us to truly understand the social and political structures and their dysfunction.

Bearing witness in the coming years may move beyond any model of satire, corporate media, as human-cyber hybridization and the rapid growth of communication technology expands with human intelligence (according to the Kurzweil model). There may always be a box for satire, but bearing witness may continue to grow into a shared experience, not necessarily geared toward advertising interests (our current state of media).

In thinking of this strategy, a new question emerges: how can media professors prepare students for new concepts of bearing witness and collaborative learning ? What new lessons can be taught using technology as a means of creating and sharing ethical encounters?

Chapter Five: On Crossing Cultures in The Cyber-Realm

SUNY Models

Media-Culture Constructs Against Interculturality
The COIL Experiment
The Henry Hudson 400 Experiment
Intercultural Communication
Homo Generator in Media Encounters

> *When you're in a different culture laughing means something different, saying hello means something different, a smile means something different, all the things that you assumed meant only one thing, you find very quickly don't mean only one thing and it kind of rocks your world, and if you're interested and curious and stable then it's an exciting experience.*
>
> –Jon Rubin, Director of the *Center for Online International Learning*, The State University of New York.

> *Then what is really important we don't know, we know we do not teach it. We also have no more a moral education which we used to teach with a certain kind of humanism and moral education. So of course education is important, is absolutely important. But how to cut into the education?*
>
> —An interview with Jean Luc Nancy by Sharif Abdunnur

Media-Culture Constructs against Interculturality

Rather than acting as a means of connecting citizens as part of a public sphere, large media outlets have turned into a consuming and invasive force, prescribing views, establishing debates and *shaping* discourse as opposed to reacting to it. In their published dialogue, Philosophy in the Present, Slavoj Zizek and Alain Badiou both contend that the terms of the American political discourse are set along lines of, what Gilles Deleuze calls, "disjunctive synthesis," as opposed to presenting terms of opposition. At the same time, the web, with over 109.5 million web sites, has become a tool of isolation--as research indicates most users only visit a handful of web sites regularly, creating 'rabbit hole' scenarios, as opposed to the *rhizomatic* (Deleuze) growth of understanding and learning in an inter-cultural cyber-realm.

In her book, *Cyber Types*, Lisa Nakamura discusses what she calls 'virtual tourism,' as a means of visiting physical locations without leaving the cyber-realm. As a critique, she adds that much of this sense of online-tourism stems from advertisers' use of exotic locales or locals from regions other than the United States, promoting *othering* (Levinas) as opposed to an open inter-cultural discourse. She indicates that this kind of thinking privileges the Western subject and his or her location. Further, she asserts that Networking ads that promise the viewer control and mastery over technology and communications discursively and visually link this power to a vision of the other which, in contrast to the mobile and networked tourist/user, isn't going anywhere (Nakamura, 2002, P. 90).

Paradoxically, the Westerner is in a fixed location, yet simultaneously the one who is on the move. What is on the line, she asserts, is diversity itself. "Diversity is displayed as the sign of that which the product will eradicate" (Nakamura, 2002, P. 88). Her critique, here, with regard to advertising in the cyber-terrain, is just. Bodies are never left behind in the cyber-realm nor are its markings. Otherness cannot simply be eradicated by capitalism on the net. What Nakamura does not offer, though, is a solution.

In his essay *Lacan Between Cultural Studies and Cognitivism*, Zizek presents distinctions in sciences and the humanities, and what he ultimately believes are false debates in cultural studies.

In our postmodernist era, that (white male/modernist) intellectual was replaced by a proliferation of theoreticians who operate in a different mode (replacing concern with one big issue with a series of localized strategic interventions), and who effectively do address issues that concern the public at large (racism and multiculturalism, sexism, how to overcome the Euro centrist curriculum, and so on) and thus trigger public debates...(Zizek, 2005, P.86)

While the critiques Nakamura offer stand, they continue the tradition of pressing against perceptions of *white-male-centrism*, but stop short of asking the larger question: "How can we change this model?" She stops at critique.

Rather than recognizing the becoming-being model, or Jean Luc Nancy's *singular-plural* as reality in the cyber-realm, or recognition of self-as-minoritarian (in Nakamura's case: becoming Asian, becoming Woman, becoming Lesbian), pressing back against the majoritarian stance, or attempting to shift majoritarian into minoritarian, her critique is stuck in neutral—never overcoming a sense of indignant undermining to move into praxis of thought, experience, action, implementation.

Against this backdrop—which includes concerns of technology, cultural demarcations, critiques without action, and the consuming edifice of mass media, and notions of curricula, where does one turn for a positive look at emerging communication technology and its uses? Where is the opportunity to foster a more individualized form of actual global communication, with the user also acting as producer, distributor, and more importantly, communicator across cultures?

Some recent experimentation with the notions of *intercultur-ality* (that is, activity between cultures with neither behaving in a privileged manner) in the communicative realms may shed light on the history of the future.

This chapter will attempt to show that the guiding principles of sovereignty (as previously outlined) and inter-cultural discourses are possible in ethical terms—providing a *smooth* space (Deleuze) for engagement.

There have been recent academy-wide experiments to bridge countries and cultures together through original web media programming, using virtual studios, or sharing media through cyber-space. Culture Studies scholar John Fisk offers that power structure is always part of cultural difference, and there are un-intended consequences of one culture colonizing another in this space, or that the stronger culture could (mis)represent the other through language or cultural difference. After this stern warning he adds, "intercultural communication is becoming more, not less, necessary for a peaceful planet" (Fiske, 2003, P.277)

Thus grappling with cultural difference on an individual level in cyberspace can be a catalyst toward exploring the dualistic meaning of communication matters.

The COIL Experiment

The Initiative

Jon Rubin, Professor of Film at The State University of New York at Purchase, recently moved away from his tenured position, to become the director of COIL: the Center for Online International Learning. This change stems from two arenas: first, his work as an artist, which, he argues, changes the context of media presentations (such as his experiments with unannounced floating cinema displays on the Hudson River), and also his work as a Fulbright scholar in Belarus for five months in 1999. While there, he taught a course called *Alternative Western Media*—the title was nearly arbitrary as his goal was to show students Western media they had not encountered before. At that point, the Belarus government had a restricted pallet of work that could be shown, and so Rubin was able to bring a wide range of work—from experimental documentaries to *The Simpsons*.

In addition, Rubin brought three little video cameras and had the students there make short videos. In a recent interview he stated that, "these were extraordinary un-technical exercises." Using an assignment from his SUNY Purchase class, Rubin had the students create 'weekend videos,' in-camera exercises that showed a slice of their lives. Rubin admits that the production values were less than stellar, but that was beside the point--he could see that they were really different from videos made by the students at Purchase.

Not because they were less technically proficient, but because they saw things differently, and even in this limited home movie modality they really chose different kind of things to shoot (Rubin).

According to Rubin, the Belarus students tended to work more metaphorically and symbolically from the second they looked through the camera. They avoided the "YouTube mode," of confessional or surface level biographical videos. These students clearly had a lot of things in their life that were difficult and complex, but culturally they were not always free to speak about. Rubin states that, "in that culture you don't go directly to the point, because going directly to the point might get you anything from fired all the way to something else, you kind of have to circle things" (Rubin).

Upon returning to Purchase, Rubin felt he was not getting the culturally complex material that he was getting abroad, and he would sometimes share his personal experience abroad that "my students didn't care about, it was not their life. And then there was this sort of revelatory moment...I showed a bunch of these videos that my Belarusian students had made."

When the lights came back on, Rubin found that the students were thoroughly engaged with this other culture. "They had a thousand questions, they were very taken with a couple of the films and a light bulb went off in my head." Rubin, realizing that this home-movie exchange was only uni-directional, decided to add another dimension. After all, if the students at Purchase were learning about the Belarusian students' life and culture by looking at their little videos, it was opening them up to the possibility that their preconception of this culture, which they "clearly thought was a bunch of old ladies picking potatoes," was based on a complete misunderstanding.

Excited by this reaction, Rubin began to develop a course module, as something sustainable—a course developed so that students in different countries would collaborate on some level or at least just exchange videos. "The problem is (in the year) 2000, it's still way pre-YouTube and the internet is around, but it's very slow...most people are still using dial-up modems." Regardless,

Rubin developed the concept for a cross-cultural video production course. The centerpiece of the course had two groups of students in two countries—they had their own classes in each country, and they mingled online in a forum while exchanging video tapes through the mail—a collaboration between two classrooms and two universities.

> And the structure that I put in place, which also I should say involved readings that had to do with culture, had to do with anthropology, had to do with media, but the primary carrot of the course was that all the students involved would make a series of videos over an entire school year, an initial iteration of it (Rubin).

The model was that every student individually would make a short video about home, about what home means to them. Rubin intentionally kept the meaning of the word "home" nebulous, so as to avoid any overly-standardized filmmaking approach.

For the American student, Rubin argues, college is a means to get away from home. For the Belarusian student it was not, so their relationship between school and home was radically different from that of the American students, but there are many other layers to it.

As the course developed, new technology allowed videos to be uploaded. At this point the challenge was bandwidth, and at European Humanities University, where the course was based in Minsk, the only way they could send videos was when the University closed in the evening at 10pm. According to Rubin, the IT technician would upload the five or six videos onto the outbound server and press the send button and by the time the University opened at seven in the morning, they would have gotten to SUNY.

When Rubin initially proposed the course at SUNY, the difficulty included the inflexibility of the conservatory structure—in other words, he had to secure his own funds via a Fulbright grant to instruct this course, while also securing funds to pay adjuncts to cover the courses he would be released from. While Rubin had the intellectual and artistic support from many on campus, there was very little fiscal support. Regardless, the course moved forward, and had an established syllabus, which involved small groups comprised of students from both countries, working on a common video narrative.

Students would spend upward of twelve weeks on a chosen theme. One student would make a short video under five minutes that was supposed to be the first scene of that video on that theme, and then their partner abroad would have two or three weeks to make the next scene and send it, and so it went .

After the grant ran out, Rubin was more and more excited about the course and indicates that students at SUNY were equally as excited about it. The next phase in this model involved the international affairs office—after all, Rubin thought, this could lead to opportunities to study abroad. The conversations in that office lead Rubin to a series of questions. "What problems emerge when sending students abroad? Who does go abroad? Who returns after a week because they're freaked out? How does this whole thing work?"

While Rubin investigated and initiated some new models, he contacted the International Programs up in Albany, and found that there were similar distance learning models, though not in video, present at other SUNY Schools—with mixed success. As Rubin piece-mailed information together, he found the next obstacle: "SUNY is not a highly networked university. It's sixty-four islands."

As technology improved, creating long-distance interactive learning models became more normative. In 2007, Rubin received a 150-thousand dollar grant from the SOROS foundation. Shortly thereafter, he received an NEH grant in 2009. But then the SUNY budget meltdown came, a ripple effect from the United States financial disaster. Though things looked bleak, Rubin was able to secure a part time assistant for additional grant writing.

With the initial start up funds depleted, Purchase was no longer interested in shouldering the initiative, so SUNY Central moved COIL's operations to the SUNY Global Center in New York City.

In January 2010 Rubin received an award from the American Council on Education, as one of four initiatives nationwide to bring technology to international education that they chose to highlight nationally. In June 2010, Rubin received a grant from the NEH to create an institute in Global Network Learning. This will allow COIL to train a group of faculty in the US and abroad to develop online/international courses in five different focus areas within the humanities.

Over the next few years, COIL has planned training conferences and capstones to present findings in international learning techniques and courses, which will be published.

Inter-culturality and Teach-able Moments.

Several questions arise as a result of the curriculum under COIL. First: is there a way to ensure that students, who may not be familiar with the adjacent culture, do not suspend empathy, or fall into a pattern of othering?

Rubin suggests that the teacher has to see it that lines of communication be opened, and if there are difficulties and frictions, the event must be turned into a "teachable moment."

As an example, Rubin offers that American students are individualistic as a culture, and are quick at this point to consider anything stereotyping. Rubin states,

In other words, you're saying that these students in Lebanon are likely to "x" or "y", well what are you talking about they each are individuals, what are you saying, you're stereotyping them. There is a real tendency for Americans, it's not entirely a bad thing, it's a good thing in many cases, to sort of say any generalization about anybody is stereotyping, but if you do that then there is no way to entertain the discussion and then so this whole issue of 'how do you see how people tend to react?' (Rubin)

In one of Rubin's classes connected with a college in Mexico, he had students from both countries post pictures of themselves as a form of identity and identification. In this particular exchange, about one third of the Mexican students showed themselves with their family, their significant other, or in a group. The American students' first reaction was that the Mexican students misunderstood the assignment, and should have just had a headshot. It did not occur to the American students' that somebody's sense of self might be bigger than their physical body, and that it might include their extended family. That in another culture they may not be isolated and see themselves as so distinct and separate. Rubin found this whole area of individualism and collectivism and how different cultures work this way. Questions of stereotyping and othering are part of the vocabulary of the classroom.

Another concern was what John Fisk warns about, cultural colonization as a result of the interaction. Though there is concern about balance in pedagogical approaches, Rubin asserts that the class is almost always initiated from the American side, or the Western side in connections between European and other nations.

In consulting with teachers about to take on course assignments that act as collaborations between the US and other nations, Rubin recalls

Although we talked about this in the prep period, like, "don't say, here's my syllabus, how are you going to work with it?" You

know what I'm saying, a rather extreme point of view anyway.
Even if you've been teaching your European History course for
twenty years, don't just walk into your partner's conversation and
say, "look at my syllabus how would you like to modify it," instead
try and start from a pre-discussion so that they have more room
to initiate. But what happened, was in general, as soon as they got
in contact with their partner, their partner was saying, "Oh, please
send me your syllabus, let me see how I can add to it. (Rubin)

In other words, their partner was totally ready to look at it from
this point of view, because they were being invited to the project
by the American side and when culturally somebody offers, the
response is to be open to the project initiator. In terms of professional development, where the Americans were trying to say, "no,
no, no you do it" and they were saying, "no, no, no we'll follow
you."

It can be culturally bound a little bit as to who defers to who
and it might be different in two different cultures.

One teachable moment Rubin describes occurred with a project between Purchase and a university in Hungary. The students
were divided as usual, with partners paring up from the separate
campuses. For this assignment, an American student videotaped
herself waking up and beginning her morning ritual: out of bed,
dressed, at the breakfast table. The Hungarian student added to
it with her ritual: out of bed, dressed, at the breakfast table. The
American student added to it: brushing teeth, and continuing
the morning ritual. The Hungarian student sent a compliment-
ary video. After a while, the American student decided to add
some humor to it, and added a title card, "My morning ritual is
better than your morning ritual." This comment was not greeted
with the intended irony, and it caused an outrage in the Hungarian
classroom—it reaffirmed the stereotype of the American stu-

dent—spoiled, lazy, without empathy, and a superior yet ignorant attitude.

For Rubin, moments like this serve as a way of navigating through further cultural misunderstanding, but not all teachable moments stem from negative encounters. One semester, one of Rubin's students had some emotional difficulty, which will not be disclosed here. As such, this student asked Rubin if he could partner off with a student in Lithuania who was not fluent in English— eliminated the chat-room and online blackboard portion of the assignment, and using the visual to communicate.   The video, which featured an egg-shaped object for both students, served as a mutual expression of artistic wonder in the midst of emotional angst. They needed no words, just, as Baudrillard would say, the *ecstasy* of communication.

Rubin states that teachers who get into it have to be open to the range of responses that can come from the people becoming cross cultural brothers and sisters to them being engaged in a wrestling match over whose perception is better and whose is right. Enough trust and enough communication need to be established so that the more troubling interactions can be addressed without meltdown. At the same time, "you don't want to protect everybody from seeing their differences." Also problems of minimization can occur, as Fisk suggests. This problem involves reducing a culture to its basic components in an effort to show that they, the other culture, are just like us.

Levinas has written at length on this topic, and although he invokes metaphysics at certain junctures, the basic message—that if the Other is not like us, we should not suspend empathy--remains.

The Henry Hudson 400 Experiment

Background

There was no textbook, by the usual definition. Certainly there have been articles, manuscripts, and tutorials that aided the process, but students and faculty from SUNY New Paltz were ultimately flying into new territory without the usual backup material to help problem-solve, or provide the comfort of guaranteed learning outcomes. Perhaps when we meet digital video production, editing, distribution, and instant feedback in the cyber realm, we are inventing the history of the future—giving students and new media makers and thinkers the ground floor of what media will ultimately be for them. When we speak about international media production and distribution, especially in a format representative of a traditional television broadcast, we are now looking beyond the large corporations, the investment in multi-million dollar studios, satellite uplinks, and even large scale production teams commonly associated with this particular aim. Also side-stepped are the commodities—the echoes of Adorno's *culture industry* that pervaded (or served as a climax to) the end of the modern period.[9] The aim of a recent assignment at The State University of New York at New Paltz was to foster a better understanding of web-media tools in the cyber-realm for college level students, while also fostering international communication across the Atlantic.

In the Spring 2009, Media Majors from the Department of Communication and Media worked in collaboration with students from InHolland University in the Netherlands. Together, they created live, interactive web television programs that were comprised of "live stand up" (in the news gathering sense), instant feedback,

---

9   Wolfgang Schirmacher discusses the close of modernity in his chapter
          on The End of Metaphysics: What does it Mean?

and pre-recorded news packages. The live portion included a div-ided screen--with New Paltz students on one side, and students from InHolland on the other side. The result was a Trans-Atlantic web-cast and subsequent documentary that *required* nobody to travel for the project. The documentary served as a climax of our collaboration, by exchanging high resolution video files through an FTP server.

This study demonstrates the kind of interactive, multi-media, international learning that the students participated in, how this kind of learning is applicable outside of this immediate discipline, and how to use these new technologies in an environment with minimal and already available resources, such as college campuses and community libraries.

The collaboration began in 2009. Four hundred years ear-lier, Henry Hudson (an Englishman sailing under the Dutch Flag on the Half-moon) traversed the Atlantic and explored the river that would later bear his name in New York State. In 2009, New York tourism promoted "Henry Hudson 400," a celebration of this journey.

As part of the celebration, an idea began to germinate in the International Affairs office at the State University of New York at New Paltz, and this is where the formal web-video and collabora-tive documentary work began. Karel Koch and Gerard Morning, professors and representatives from InHolland University in The Netherlands met with professors at New Paltz, and laid the groundwork for what was to follow: four live news magazine style webisodes and a longer form documentary. The mission was to use available resources and technology, while creating a teachable product for students and faculty members. At the same time, the content would celebrate Dutch entrepreneurship and influence in the New York region—an influence that still exists today.

The Webisodes

The first step was the introduction between the students at InHolland and in New Paltz. This was a positive first step, as it allowed immediate conversations using the Skype interface. Through this interface, the students formulated 'themes' upon which each episode would explore. From there, each team (InHolland and New Paltz) created several news packages that described the theme. For instance, one theme was 'Water as Place.' For this, students created a package in which folk singer and professor Harry Stoneback was interviewed, in which he discussed his song about the Hudson River. The song sold millions of copies—in China. The question became why? Why did a song that celebrated an eastern American river meet with commercial success in China, while remaining relatively unknown in New York? This video package, which ran about four minutes, became embedded in the live, 30-plus minute program, which also included additional pre-created packages by both student groups, and 'live' conversation before and after each segment was web-cast.

Students used the make.tv interface, which boasts a virtual studio and switcher, a reduced version of what one may expect to find in a traditional television control room. There is a virtual preview monitor, media available for playback, and an interface to allow camera inputs. They signed in, using the account created by the students in The Netherlands, to ensure they were sharing the same space.

In any kind of experimentation, there are a variety of understood variables for outcomes. The expected technical outcomes are fairly basic with regard to overall quality of the product. To say that the initial episode was inelegant is a polite understatement. Despite a rigorous rehearsal, the time delay was exacerbated to a greater degree this time, perhaps due to unknown variables taking place within the server, itself. (It should be noted that in order to move our signal from the SONY HDV camera to the computer, make.tv required an additional Flash 2.5 plug in for its interface—this also could be the culprit).

While the half-hour episode ran at thirty-eight minutes, and included dead air, shots of students unaware that the show was going on live at that moment, and some cluttered communication, humor saved the day! That is to say that the students seem to find the thrill of experimentation to be more rewarding than a sharp product for consumption—it was in the dialogue between the students on both sides of the ponds that a truer collegiality occurred, and the program was simply a conduit to this end.

The students adjusted for the problems encountered during the initial episode, and using a floor manager on Skype (rather than attempting the www.make.tv talkback), time delays and other problems were anticipated, and dealt with, for cleaner professional products.

With the webisodes completed in the summer of 2009, several students remained dedicated to the next leg of the project: creating a fifteen-minute personal profile documentary about Dutch entrepreneurs in New York. Three people were profiled: an architect, a fashion designer, and a sound designer/ audio engineer. Much of the footage was captured and edited by our Dutch Colleagues (primarily by Jerry Loos of Loos films), and the New York footage was captured by New Paltz student Dan Butler. Dan shot, then cut together, cityscapes and scenes to act as b-roll for the documentary, sharing footage by exporting Mp4 files over the Filezilla FTP (a free download).

As a climax to our collaboration, the Dutch students and professors flew to New York—visiting New Paltz, and then organizing a premiere of the documentary at a rooftop party in Manhattan. The students who had all collaborated on the project were able to finally meet face to face after working for months on end in the cyber terrain.

The Outcome

Many texts and studies have proclaimed 'it can be done,' in the cyber-realm, and spotlighting the technical process may help embolden those who are rightfully critical of the media to learn first-hand alternatives to mass consumption. The next part is to lay out the theoretical learning outcomes. In interviews with the eight participating New Paltz students afterwards, the consensus was that they felt more effective as communicators, due in large part to this process.

When creating the webisodes and the documentary with the college in The Netherlands, there were a few elements already in place that assisted the dialogue. For starters, the argument the pieces were making, which has been echoed by a number of local scholars including Fran Dunwell, is that the Dutch have had a profound cultural impact on New York, and in the communities along the Hudson much of that impact has echoed. Dunwell makes the argument that New York's traditionally American Left leaning view (even in the face of a national swing to the American Right), is in part due to The Netherland's more liberal culture reverberations. With that, there was already groundwork for the dialogue laid between the two participating universities, New Paltz and InHolland.

With the example of a 'teachable moment' Rubin points out that no such groundwork has been laid. The experiment is, in part, without the safety net of pre-existing media influence.

Intercultural Communication

Rubin showed an episode of *The Simpsons* to his students in Belarus. The episode was about radioactive pollution, and this is a country that was affected by Chernobyl. It is conceivable that some of the students in the class were injured by Chernobyl's fallout when they were children due to the timing of their birth and that event. Rubin claims this was not in the foreground of his thinking when he screened the episode,

> ...but I wasn't unaware of it either, showing it, I don't know how to put it, to say they were in shock is not correct, but they were deeply affected by this slightly humorous show because it was stuff that wasn't spoken of in that way there and it took a tone that was very critical of industry and government that *The Simpsons'* tends to be and the level of irony that was there was unusual for them and they really reacted to that particular *Simpsons* episode like it was a revelation that people could publicly, on television, be so critical of what was going on around them, which was difficult in this culture to do. (Rubin)

The culture had been a more controlled culture, and these kinds of interactions across country borders can lead to larger consequences. In 2004 the institution in Belarus was shut down by the government, which had a harsh reaction against liberal universities bringing Western lecturers onto their campuses—more and more the government had been putting pressure on the university to not function the way they wanted to function.

A few weeks after Rubin finished the 2004 course, troops were sent, the university was physically shut down, and the students were thrown out. It was just shut down. Rubin says, "this was a horrible thing although you could sort of see it coming; I mean I

wasn't that surprised when it happened, although it was still horrible, and of course the American students who had been collab-
orating with these Belarusian students just weeks before, although
it was summer break for them, getting this email from saying, "by
the way, all your buddies are no longer at the university."

Rubin expresses that this was a wake up call for the American
students who "sit around having beers, complaining about a paper,
they don't worry about troops coming in and throwing them out
on the street." To be fair, it is not a model that Rubin or anyone
else wishes to replicate, but there was no escaping this reality.

Two years later, the university in Belarus secured additional
western funding, which in fact was part of the reason the government distrusted the institution so much, to reopen in Lithuania,
as a university in exile. Lithuania is the adjoining country and
Vilnius, where they are set is only a three hour train ride or bus
ride from Minsk. "So it was close enough that students and faculty
could go back and forth and this new university had been created."

Rubin still occasionally works with this University in Exile
through the COIL model.

Homo Generator in Cyber Encounters

On the European Graduate School web site, Wolfgang Schirmacher
offers this idea about media creators in the 21st Century:

> Media creators need to be bold thinkers, capable of inventing frame-
> works and designing artificial life. Uncertainty is the beginning. In
> an ever-changing information society, the crucial skill is a kind of
> thinking which explores openness and challenges our fear of the un-
> known. In the age of media, knowledge has become information, an
> all too perishable commodity. Hence, only questions have kept their
> defining power. (Schirmacher)

The media creator in the twenty first century is one engaged in autopoiesis—the new media maker is very much homo generator, making themselves, moving beyond any previously established model, and media educators must recognize this for their students to engage in ethical encounters in the cyber-realm.

This moves us beyond the striated space of otherness from demarcations of gender, ethnicity, sexual orientation, or physical borders on the map. This is smooth and nomadic space (Deleuze/ Guattarri), and a space to move beyond faciality as a means of *othering* a non-western culture.

Convergence. Interdisciplinary. We've heard these words before. At best, they can serve as a model for fostering intercultural understanding across a variety of curricula at the university level. At worst, they are catch phrases, searching for practical application amidst academic climates striving to stay current in the face of budget woes.

These words only morph in the coming generation into a very basic understanding: media. Media technology, in particular the cyber realm, has moved our thinking away from the traditional large models of media-making. We are, however, at a crossroads. On one hand there is the thrill of the experiment, the thrill of the new frontier the cyber-realm provides for the individual to be their own international news gatherer, with peers in other states, nations, continents, hemispheres. What better way to instruct students about the necessity for intercultural communication than with assignments that do just that?

It really means that the two faculty members, the co-teachers have to explore a set of issues themselves pretty carefully and that doesn't mean it's just for self protection, so that the expectations of the faculty and the students are set at a reasonable place and this has to be both with technology issues and with issues of classroom behavior, of what's acceptable, and without being too restrictive, without tying everybody in a straight jacket. COIL, which is still an evolving piece, is laying out a series of questions and a table that two people could use even though it's a work in progress to sort of help self-identify specific places where these issues might come up, some of which, one might be very aware of up front and others one might not have even thought of but they could still erupt. Their attempt is to gradually help people prepare for these so that when there are conflicts they are useful or at least teachable issues and not just meltdowns.

The intercultural interactions are necessary, those that move past demarcations, but some sceptics and scepticism remains. Lisa Nakamura reasserts her claim that the demarcations are real and being monetized, and those who push against this are waging a fool's war.

Libertarian rhetoric, such as that often seen in *Wired* magazine's editorials, is apt to display a more radical optimism; its maxim that "information wants to be free" assumes that freeing the information by making it available on the Net will liberate users from their bodies and hence from inconvenient side effects such as racism and sexism. (Nakamura, 2002, P. 107)

She goes on to fight against this notion, and points to multiple examples of racism, and sexism, from racial role playing in cyberspace (which reaffirms old stereotypes) to even more horrendous notions of wiping out race entirely" (Ibid). It is not an argument of erasing race, gender, or identification entirely—it's a matter of moving past otherness as a means for rejecting those before you. As Judith Butler states at the end of her section on *Responsibility* in her work:

> Perhaps most importantly, we must recognize that ethics requires us to risk ourselves precisely at moments of unknowingness, when what forms us diverges from what lies before us, when our willingness to

become undone in relation to others constitutes our chance of becoming human. To be undone by another is a primary necessity, an anguish, to be sure, but also a chance—to be addressed, claimed, bound to what is not me, but also to be moved, to be prompted to act, to address myself elsewhere, and so to vacate the self-sufficient "I" as a kind of possession. If we speak and try to give an account from this place, we will not be irresponsible, or, if we are, we will be surely forgiven (Butler, 2005, P. 136).

PART THREE: Bodily Living and Homo Generator Aesthetics As Models for Sovereignty in Singularity

Chapter Six: On Media Tactility & Sexuality in the Cyber-Realm

Introduction: Moving past the Adult Entertainment Industry
The Electronic Orgasm
The Sexual Identity Aesthetic
The Sexual Identity Non-History
Giving an Account of Oneself in Sexual Aporias
Conclusion: Bodily Living In the Cyber-Realm as a
   Sexual Being

We have reached a fateful turning-point in contemporary culture when human sexuality is a killing-zone, when desire is fascinating only as a sign of its own negation, and when the pleasure of catastrophe is what drives ultramodern culture onwards in its free fall through a panic scene of loss, cancellation, and exterminism.

—Kroker, *Body Invaders, Panic Sex in America*, 1987

This, precisely, is the mark of the perfect style in each and every art: that it is able to remove the specific limitations of the art in question without thereby destroying its specific qualities, and through a wise use of its individual peculiarities, is able to confer upon it a more general character.

–Schiller, *Letters on Aesthetics*, Second Letter, Paragraph Four

Introduction: Moving Past the Adult Entertainment Industry

In a 2000 *Simpsons* episode, "Fatih Off", Homer Simpson re-turns to his alma-matter. Upon meeting his former roomies, all of whom are *stereotyped* in a Stephen Hawking convention, one of his old buddies informs him that his research in technology will allow a computer-user to download porn "a million times faster." To which, Homer drools, "..a...million...times" (IMDB, 2010) We laugh, in part, because of the reality of sexual imagery in media, and its accessibility in cyber space.

Sexting. Chat Roulette. IBOD. It seems every time a cyber-netizen enters the cyber-realm, new innuendo or sexual activity emerges, including random imagery of the nude male showcasing his genitalia for chat roulette. If something *can* be sexualized, it *will* be. In the consideration of mediated sexual encounters, the cyber-realm is in a sense a pioneer in several areas, including that of interactive tactility through the IBOD.

Tracing human sexuality along with erotic artifice, we can examine erotic pottery, erotic poetry, paintings, pictures, photos, and eventually movies—from those viewed in *blue* cinemas to those consumed in a home theater environment.

Simulated sexual encounters, the whispered conversation or innuendo, took a more abrupt form through phone sex—either enjoyed by couples at a distance or as a phone sex service for a fee as a form of virtual sex. Virtual sex in the cyber-realm takes the form of quick videos, longer videos, one-on-one dialogue in chat rooms, to virtual sex with avatars—think of *the Sims*, but xxx rat-ed. This also includes new business models in "saving" the adult entertainment industry—or at least new models in monetizing the business.

Much like other capitalistic enterprises, the adult entertainment industry faces the next evolution—if a person no longer needs to leave their home to purchase a DVD or a video, and can download clips for free or at a moderate price online, then where does that leave the industry? A recent Current TV news piece suggested the adult entertainment industry could be reinvigorated by social networking (Vanguard Documentary Current TV, 2010). In the piece, which aired as part of the *Vanguard Documentary* series, an adult video star, Jessica Drew, showcased her latest marketing technique—every morning, she takes a picture of herself in bed. She takes a picture of herself in her car, eating lunch, going to the set. She tweets, updates her status across social media sites, and has her own site as well to showcase more personal content, for a more direct connection with her fan base.

Rather than adult entertainment remaining purely in the realm of fantasy, the line dividing the adult oriented fantasy from the real (i.e., the character separate from the performer), there has in this case been a total eradication of the private, the public, the performance, and the inter-active—as Baudrillard suggested in *The Ecstasy of Communication*, the separation between public and private has evaporated due to our mediated encounters (*Baudrillard*, 1993 p.131).

A separate *Vanguard Documentary* on the same cable network showcased a number of adult entertainment industry workers (not just actors, but crews as well), who were being given health benefits, and learning additional skills by marketing their fantasy products in a heavily competitive marketplace (Vanguard Documentary Current TV, 2010). In other words, as part of the investigative item, the storyline glamorized those working behind the scenes, perhaps to attract new technological innovators to join in their business ventures. The innovators would be responsible for moving the technology faster, while also offering new platforms for interaction. "There's always a new day, a new format, a new device," offers Nicole to the Current TV interviewer. Nicole's professional title is 'Broadcast Engineer, Kink.com.' *Wired* magazine editor Regina Lynn offers that 'we are a tool centered species, we're very creative...and we're horny' (Vanguard Documentary Current TV, 2010). Part of the technological upkeep and expediency has to do with cleaner video codecs, faster processors, and faster connections to the internet, but also the heterotopia (Foucault) of encounters in the realm. How does one 'push the envelope,' not only in terms of content, but also in the experience being offered? How personalized can this be?

Of course, the tragic irony (perhaps) is that the adult entertainment industry is currently suffering as part of its early success. The early adopters of new technology tend to be those who are interested in faster connection to sexual imagery or virtual experiences, and while that has driven the price down for technology due to the economies of scale personal computers, it has also driven profits down as well. Democratizing sleaze.

Consider this snapshot:
- 43 percent of all internet users look at pornography. This measurement is taken by IP address, and does not take into account that those at work are not able to view pornographic material for fear of losing their jobs in a variety of sectors.
- One out of every three porn viewers is female.
- The average time a person spends looking at pornography on the web is fifteen minutes.
- China and South Korea have the largest porn revenues, with the United States trailing at 14 percent.
- 35 percent of all downloads are pornographic
- The United States spends 13.6 billion on porn (From Current. com, 2010)

These numbers, though, are actually down (Current.com, 2010). What is not addressed in these numbers or in the *Vanguard Documentary* pieces is why the adult industry exists and survives

as an enterprise to begin with—beyond the basic taboo of titilla-
tion. The industry EXISTS in large part due to the marginalization
of –as Zizek would offer—*the real* (Zizek, 2005). The conversation
about sexuality, sexual imagery, and sexual identity still remains
in the outer-fringes—despite progress (political progress, social
progress) being made, true explorations of sexuality and sexual
identity (separate yet connected) are met as taboo and therefore
sidelined. The surface dialogue as enacted by the mass media
seems to fall into the safety net of *what about the children?* (Parents
Television Council, 2010) In other words, they warn, do not talk
about it.

   In part, this sidelining has allowed the adult industry to
exist—for if acceptance of the broadest possible spectrum of sexual identities and culture became normative, the market value of
monetizing sexuality would be reduced, if not altogether taken
away from industrial/capitalistic hierarchy. As filmmaker Barbara
Hammer wrote, "If erotic expression were supported in our culture…there would be a diminution of pornography." (Hammer,
P.200, 2010)

The Electronic Orgasm

The historiography connecting technology and sexuality is not a
new exploration, but the model has been rife with misunderstand-
ings, while also creating opportunities for proper subversion. In a
PBS interview in the early 1970s, theorist Lewis Mumford, whose
Technics and Civilization (Mumford, 1963) became a cornerstone
for Marshall McLuhan's research, told interviewer Bill Moyers
that man's technological pursuit was being done purely for 'the
electronic orgasm' (PBS, 1972). The formulator of technics at that
point felt that the new fangled technology, with an eye toward
immediacy without concerns of cultural consequence, was vain

to the point of being purely masturbatory. A life-long student of technology, Mumford turned his back on anything electronic in his later years—he became a neo-luddite, living in Amenia, New York, in a country home with a gas oven, and a non-electronic typewriter to assist with his later essays and correspondences.

This is a rather large rejection from a scholar referenced so vividly not only by McLuhan, but also Neil Postman—in particular with his amendment to the theory of technics, titled *Technopoly*[10] (Postman, 1993). Mumford saw several connections between the expedience of technological development and cultural narcissism; technical virtuosity in the service of cretinism.

The connection Mumford did not make was the suppression of sexuality in the larger mass culture (even after the supposedly open 1960s in the United States) lead to two particular forms of identity reorientation: the first was the expedited capitalistic selling of sexuality in advertisements and in mass media—reaffirming gender roles and reinstituting the subject/object debate.   The second form arrived as a reaction against this commodification of sexuality and sexual identity. Both Kenneth Anger and Barbara Hammer turned the camera onto their own perceptions (and in Barbara Hammer's case, herself), in order to fill a void, and make an abrupt and unapologetic entrance into the public sphere per their sexual identities (a gay man, and a lesbian respectively). After all, if the media were portraying women as either Mrs. Cunningham in *Happy Days*, or Farah Fawcett's Jill Munroe in *Charlie's Angels*, where could the "alternative lifestyle," such as those lived by Hammer and Anger be seen and enacted?

With the above information as a backdrop for where sexual-

---

10   In fairness, this is a reductive view of Technopoly, but the main crux is in large part an expansion and problematization of Mumford's work. It should also be noted that Postman's work had a more critical reading of media and technology than Mumford's.

ity in the cyber-realm is today, a glance backward toward media installations that recognized immediate connections between sexuality, the body as politics, and technology will be discussed, followed by a glance forward toward new models of hybrid bio-technical apparati in erotic artifice and being-becoming. Several key points will surface, entwining thoughts put forth by Deleuze and Guattarri, Wolfgang Schirmacher, Donna Haraway, Roland Barthes, and finally the politics of the aesthetic body, through the examination of Barbara Hammer's and Judith Butler's work. Jacques Ranciere offers a succinct starting point-- "Politics exists when the figure of a specific subject is constituted, a supernumerary subject in relation to the calculated number of groups, places, and functions in a society" (Ranciere, 2006, P. 51)

Sexual Identity Aesthetic

Moving beyond the adult entertainment industry and numbers, *the desire process* as defined by Deleuze and Guattari exists and connects to axioms outside of fulfillment, and continues to be entwined with being and becoming—also understood in this paradigm as process, and a simultaneous occurrence without arrival. In this case, that process is one of sexual identity and sexual desire/expression.

Ultimately, taking sexuality and expressions of sexual identity away from the adult industry and into the public sphere would result in one of the largest political and social actions imaginable: total authority over our sex, and sexuality—our sovereignty as sexual beings. This is not a call against fantasy, or for adult-related media content being screened during children's viewing hours, but rather a simple recognition that sexual (mis)understanding and exploration often occurs at junctures that do not offer a real picture of identity. It is a call to push against marginalization. Technology, the politics of the body, and the eroticism of sexuality entwine in the formation of a sexual identity aesthetic.

In her book, *Hammer: Making Movies Out of Sex and Life*, Barbara Hammer refers to herself as "an experimental filmmaker and lesbian feminist" (Hammer, 2010, P.200). This statement begins her chapter titled *The Politics of Abstraction*, in which she further asserts that "radical content deserves radical form," and continues her autobiography pointing out key productions of hers that support this thesis.

Her body of work, which features in great detail her body proper, offers images and sounds that confront the audience with a new sexual aesthetic—that of sexual identity, sexuality, sexual exploration, and the abrupt confrontation to the mass-mediated image of woman as subservient to patriarchy.

Her film work invites activity, made explicit by the raw imagery, plays on temporality, and vivid portrayals of sexuality. The erotic, the tactile, is closely coupled with a call against censorship by "parents and patriarchs," and liberation of self as such. Expounding upon a bodily-pleasure motif that arrives from both love-making and filmmaking, Hammer offers,

> Lesbian sexuality is directly connected to lesbian art making. In fact, lovemaking and art making are interchangeable pleasurable activities. The sense of the erotic in art making is a sense of wholeness, of completeness, of building from beginnings to finishings, making for an awesome and wonderful sense of fullness of being. (Hammer, 2010, P. 119)

In her language concerning *being*, her choice of the word 'fullness,' indicates a motion that stems from a state of incompleteness, or rather *becoming*. Deleuze and Guattari offer notions of becoming in *A Thousand Plateaus*. "Becoming is a verb with a consistency all its own; it does not reduce to, lead back to, appearing,' 'being,' equaling or 'producing' (Deleuze and Guattari, 1987, P. 239). This form of becoming is a reference to the larger apparatus, the axioms of process that permeate political structures and anti-structures. Through this process, they identify two forms in the politics of becoming: Majoritarian, and Minoritarian. Majoritarian refers to a state of domination, and how a man constitutes himself in the grid of things. Minoritarian stems from the concept of social minority. The term suggests, among other things, marginalized political and social ideologies such as Hammer's. While the majoritarian position is not one that self arises, or authoritarian by premade structure, Deleuze and Guattari do not draw the conclusion that it must be battled against. Rather, as all is process and all is becoming, their desire is to transform the majoritarian position into minoritarian. Through this passage, they offer up the concepts of the whole, and the particle-d (or molecular). Hammer's politics, in this instance, are part of the molecular formation, making chains, connections, and further axioms.

These becomings as process then must push against what they call the arboreal or tree-like understandings of political and social hierarchy, and embrace the rhizomatic, the model of growth comparable to grass growing in a field, spreading out as a multi-plateau.

With the language of majoritarian and minoritarian, that is becoming-woman: "There is no becoming-majoritarian; majority is never becoming" (Deleuze and Guattari, 1987, P. 106). So, all becoming is minoritarian.

The becoming, then, is a state of the transitory, and the state of process as recognition. It is a call to the sexed subjectivity, one of gender and gender troubles of identity, as put forth by Judith Butler. It is a call to move beyond traditionally structured self in opposition to other paradigms, embracing difference and Derrida's notion of Differànce that recognizes becoming woman, becoming lesbian, becoming feminist.

In merging notions of becoming woman with Barbara

Hammer's work, Hammer offers her perception that,

> Woman must write woman. Woman must film woman. Any censorship, any confusion of sexuality and pornography, and fear to treat the taboo topic, not to claim our bodies ourselves, will further silence one half of the peoples of the world, will inhibit, and worse, prohibit our species' liberation (Hammer, 2010, P. 123)

In her chapter, *For an Active Cinema*, Hammer frames her work as the intermediary between politics and feminism, through art. She argues for what she calls *an active cinema*.

Active cinema is a cinema where the audience is engaged physically, involved with a sense of their bodies as they watch the screen. In passive cinema the audience is a spectator to the whims and fancies of the director...Active cinema is not an escape. It is its own experience. (Hammer, 2010, P.128)

Hammer notes the prominence of self-reflexivity in her work, from the subversive ruptures that punctuate *History Lessons*, to the over-intentionality of the camera's known presence in *Optic Nerve*. "At no time does active cinema intend to mystify the means used to obtain the image nor disarm or obfuscate the audience" (Hammer, 2010, P.123).

The self-reflexivity is a characteristic of much of her work, in particular during the 1980s. In *Sync Touch*, the image seems to run off the reels; she creates images of herself spooning a 16mm camera in her bed. The interplay of self-love, mediated love, and reflexivity resituates notions of female identity and sexuality in a technological and mediated embrace.

If, as Hammer puts forth, "art and politics go hand in hand," (Hammer, 2010, P.128) what are the politics of *No Nooky TV*, a 1988 16mm project that focuses on physical love as capitulated with technology?

In keeping with Deleuze and Guattari, and their notion of the particl-d, the molecular strain grows out of her self-identification as a lesbian feminist, through the film. The film opens with a black screen, with a computer-altered (or perhaps generated) masculine voice, stating "I have a man's voice....by appropriating me women will have a voice."

"The voice" that needs to be re-appropriated in order for the woman to have a voice is masculine, subverted by woman in identity formation. This notion operates as a literal device, as this voice (presumably) Hammer speaks through is masculine—and also operates as a political device as she asserts her own subjectivity through the re-appropriation. What is being held in tension here is the interplay of understood identifiers.

The space, all dark, all encompassing, is temporal and shifted by the quick dissolve, scored by simple computer generated music. An image of a computer monitor appears, and on that monitor there are some shifting graphics. Female line drawn figures are electronically created on the screen. For the first minute, a series of words appear along with this music before the first subversive rupture: the sound of an urgent telephone tone—as though an unseen phone were left dangling off the hook. Communication is broken, and something new arrives out of the rupture. Text that reads:

"Does she like me? WANT ME? DESIRE ME? KILL FOR ME? LUST FOR ME?"

Another rupture, the sound of an internal fax modem connecting, with the words:

"SHE CALLED SHE CALLED.

"Didn't know if she wanted art or love.

"SHE CAN HAVE BOTH."

At this point the imagery, text, and sounds form an ecology of sexual enticement between partners, as all the mediated content within the piece grow in urgency. A soundscape of a cheerful woman, as she describes a sexual encounter with another woman, more noise and computer generated sounds add to the terrain, and the visuals shift on—giving a sense of uncertain ground until a connection is made.

At first, flirtatious messages appear on the computer screen. Some are romantic and whimsical, others become more heated— more direct. Barbara Hammer appears at the eighth minute of the film, anointing herself with 'oil of Lesbos,' according to the monitor—rubbing her face with an electronic device while seated in front of the active computer screen.

While we do not see another character in the film outside of Hammer (unless the computer can be considered a character), the immediate information we can glean gives us a sense of engendering. For instance, the computer screen reads, 'Let's Jack Off' at one moment—and then a response appears on an adjacent screen, "Jill Off Dear!" Jack, acting as a proper name in this case, is a misnomer due to its masculine identification. This act, then, is not a cyber-encounter over a computer between a woman and a man, but between two women. Although there is a computer jack present, its role as metaphor is being subverted out of the masculine construct.

When describing the piece in her book, she contends, "I questioned what lesbian identity and representation meant and put these ideas into practice one summer playing with a new girlfriend and an Amiga computer" (Hammer, 2010, P. 145).

As mentioned, we do not see the "new girlfriend," it at first seems unclear exactly who this encounter is with, though we know from the descriptors that the other is certainly female. As the film climaxes, Hammer, nude on her bed, pleasures herself with an electronic device, though a distinct impression is made—that the computer may in fact be connected to the device, and therefore acting as her lover.   A singularity in lovemaking.

Throughout her book Hammer comments on her images of lesbian lovemaking on the screen, as well as her own appearances, often nude, in an embrace. In her section on *For an Active Cinema,* she speaks of woman loving woman as a form of 'self loving.'

> Self loving is a repossession of the wholeness and goodness of woman before patriarchal myths, before our existence, before we inherited a planet where to be a girl was to be secondary. If the audience can sense the self-loving of the women on the screen, they can activate their personal self-loving. Woman-defined erotic cinema invites an active audience (Hammer, P.130, 2010).

The intentionality blends concepts around self-love, lesbian love-making, and sex with/through technology, and also lends itself to the paratext: the ecology between text and image.

At once we understand the computer, the technology, the images on the screen, with the hyper-flashing messages, encouraging the user to continue in the loving text, the larger fonts, and more explicit comments. Gender resituates itself in the images on the monitor—going so far as to wear women's underwear at one point, evoking Donna Haraway's *Cyborg Manifesto* as a radical statement against altruistic gender and gender norms, and the separation of flesh and machine—or in the words of Wolfgang Schirmacher, the "biological tyranny." (Schirmacher, Networld)

Haraway's seminal text on cyborgs begins with her desire to "build an ironic political myth faithful to feminism, socialism, and materialism" (Haraway, Cyborg). In doing so, she constructs her "blasphemy," the Cyborg. This metaphor serves as a means to move past traditional boundaries between man and woman, living and artificial, and reclaims the cybernetic image from the masculine gaze. Hammer's reclaiming of the computer-generated masculine voice intersects with Haraway's Cyborg image—which had been made popular in the 1980s by the film *The Terminator,* featuring the masculine icon Arnold Schwarzenegger.

The images, in particular those that sexualize the computer monitor, offer a transcendence of the image, and the interplay of what Roland Barthes called the *Studium* and *Punctum.*

The *studium*, as Barthes offers, is "(an) application to a thing, taste for someone, a kind of general enthusiastic commitment, of course, but without special acuity" (Barthes, 1981, P. 26). The *punctum*, on the other hand, is the "element that will break (or punctuate) the *studium*...it also refers to the notion of punctuation" (Barthes, 1981, P. 26).
"The studium is always coded. The punctum is not" (Barthes, 1981, P. 26).

In situating these terms further, Barthes offers his encounters with Mapplethorpe's photographs of Robert Wilson and Philips Glass.

> Wilson *holds* me, though I cannot say why, *i.e.,* say *where*: is it the eyes, the skin, the position of the hands, the track shoes? The effect is certain but unlocatable, it does not find its sign, its name; it is sharp and yet lands in a vague zone of myself; it is acute yet muffled, it cries out in silence. (Barthes, 1981, P. 53)

Bringing the *studium* to Hammer's work is a subjective experience—what in the image, the laying of images in an extended dissolve, immediately presents itself in the category? Is it the familiarity of the computer monitor? The *affection-image*--to further evoke Deleuze as she massages her face with the electronic device? Is it the candid and uncensored nature of her appreciation of a lover and self through technology? These elements are all immediately striking, and in the present. What lingers or is revealed later?

In a more specific demonstration of *punctum*, Barthes offers, the *punctum* should be revealed only after the fact, when the photograph is no longer in front of me and I think back on it. "I may know better a photograph I remember than a photograph I am looking at, as if direct vision oriented its language wrongly, engaging it in an effort of description which will always miss its point of effect, the *punctum*" (Barthes, 1981, P. 53).

Appreciation of the *studium* in this case occurs in the joy of Hammer's intentionality of meaning through imagery. The interplay of animated images on the screen recalls cyber-interactions in its infancy, and a kind of playfulness through the animation programs. The *punctum*, on the other hand, arrives in those subversive ruptures—the moments that shake the audience out of a 'settling into' the visuals and sounds. Barthes evaluated still images with this taxonomy, though the *punctum* in Hammer's work arrives in those moments that interrupt the visual narrative in the temporality.

The lovemaking in the film moves beyond physical sexuality, as the words convey deeply felt emotions between lovers. There are illustrations of lines, making connections between phrases, perhaps connecting Hammer with her love on the other side of the screen, or with the computer itself. The computer is no longer a tool, it is living, responding, accelerating. Being with Hammer's body. Sense of location, or that of landscape are jutted out—the images become increasingly layered, and Hammer's movements are sped up as she interacts more intimately with the technology. Haraway suggests,

> Only by being out of place could we take intense pleasure in machines, and then with excuses that this was organic activity after all, appropriate to females. Cyborgs might consider more seriously the partial, fluid, sometimes aspect of sex and sexual embodiment. (Haraway, Cyborg)

Lesbian lovemaking and lovemaking through technology as an act of *love*, in keeping with the notion of *punctum* further serves as a binding agent between aesthetics and politics. Expanding upon creating *No Nooky TV*, Hammer writes,

> Although the 80s were a conservative time, ideas of social construction of almost anything were in the air. This was liberating for me as I thought about the social construction of lesbians (Hammer, 2010 P. 145)

To add to this concept, that of social construction of sexuality, Judith Butler problematized normative and non-normative categorizations with her work, <u>Gender Trouble</u>, a work published within a few years of *Cyborg Manifesto* and within a few years of the screening of *No Nooky TV* .

The Sexual Identity Non-History

Butler suggests that trans-sexuality, homo-sexuality, and subversive performative roles have eroded previously understood hetero-normative values as self-evident—that sexual identity politics, and sexuality itself is greatly performative.

Both Butler and Hammer post the questions in their work: Who counts as real or who has recognizable gender? Who has recognizable sexual orientation? Gender as understood by Butler and Haraway, seems to exist without the need for the body. In the words of Haraway, "Gender might not be global identity after all, even if it has profound historical breadth and depth" (Haraway, Cyborg).

In consideration of *historicity*, in particular the definition as explored by Jacques Ranciere which in part materializes recorded political history vis-à-vis aesthetics, Barbara Hammer's work makes material an ignored subject: that is, Lesbian contribution to the milieu. Her written work warns against censorship (both in the arenas of art and history) and brings lesbian history into frame, and her film work acts as a means of making this tactile.

In the absence of a sutured and taught history, Barbara Hammer created several pieces, including *Nitrate Kisses* and *History Lessons*. Both films explore lesbian sexuality in history, the latter also providing a satirical lens to stock footage, the archival collage to create not a sutured history, but a mosaic of gesture in historical recognition. The aim, as Hammer states, was to "take film clips of lesbian representation made by men from the beginning of the twentieth century until Stonewall and turn them into comedic sequences[11]" (Hammer, 2010 P. 227). She also contends that lesbians must "write, photograph, film our sexuality, because it's one of the bases of our new language" (Hammer, 2010, P.131).

Throughout Hammer's work, she argues that lesbians-in-history, and lesbians-as-history (minoritarian) have never received the kind of encyclopedic treatment that white-hetero history has received (the majoritarian). Haraway supports this view, when she says, "Our bodies, ourselves; bodies are maps of power and identity...Up till now (once upon a time), female embodiment seemed to be given, organic, necessary; and female embodiment seemed to mean skill in mothering and its metaphoric extensions." Hammer's aesthetic, the *studium*, the *punctum*, the particl-d exploration, the subversive ruptures, the love-making, the technology, weaves to form a sovereign image of identity. The sexual identity aesthetic.

This aesthetic--which in part includes Hammer's quest to explore lesbian history through film--suggests, though, that history can at times be a mirage. Indeed, one must be careful of a history

---

11   It should also be noted that the film's original title was 'Porn Doctor,' but her production grant was nearly pulled as there was an objection to the use of the word 'porn' in the title.

that seems too sutured together, as this tends not to be the actuality of history, but of an attempt to neatly compartmentalize events. As though one sprang catalyst from the previous—or as Michael Anker would suggest--"there is no point of origin in the sense that each origin erases itself in dissemination" (Anker, 2009, P.13).

Giving an Account of Oneself in Sexual Aporias

In his book, *The Ethics of Uncertainty: Aporetic Openings*, Michael Anker lists ten possible meanings for a philosophical notion: "as something is coming to be it is always already becoming something other" (Anker, 2009, P.13). Anker calls upon Nietzsche and Derrida, and their use of the word 'origin.' The argument that emerges is that 'origin' is misused as a fixed starting point in or of temporality as opposed to one that "describes, on the contrary, a movement of language" (Anker, 2009, P. 13).

Origin, in other words, cannot free temporality and be a priori, as one event becomes the next, leaving as it is becoming, without a demarcation. In gender, the phenomenon of *trans* has become a locus for aporetic openings and deciphering—on one hand, the *trans* as a state of being, indicates in between states, or in between states of becoming, and is in itself a state of becoming. Throughout much of her work, Judith Butler focused on the idea of becomings as precarious life. She suggests that the decision to become "transman" is not necessarily rooted in terms of repudiating one's gender; that there might be something positive in working through this issue has largely been ignored.

Recently, Judith Butler recalled an event that took place in northern California. At a slam event in San Francisco titled ""Transgender and the 'Spirit of Revolt': Reflections on Melancholic Rage," a young trans-gendered poet (female to male) spoke out against the notion of transient sexuality with a fervent 'fuck you' to Judith Butler in his verse, unaware that Butler was in the audience. Moments later, Judith Butler herself approached the poet, thanked him for the poem, and added (after there was apparently no recognition) "I'm Judith Butler" (Fitzpatrick, 2007).

The poet rejected "Butler" (not necessarily the person as much as her work on gender) for Butler's suggestion of gender fluidity, which works against his own desire to be recognized as the masculine part of a binary sex system. Still, this adds to the uncertain and open aporia of gender identification between groups who desire recognition, those who desire autonomy, those with a voice, those without—and how to make connections between that are not simply arbitrary assertions.

In her work *Giving An Account of Oneself* (2005) Judith Butler brings together Adorno, Levinas, Foucault, Freud and others in grappling with ideas of identity and responsibility. As she attempts to bring forth self knowledge, she at times reiterates theoretical postulations that the self exists, in part, in relation to something else. In her passage on "Foucaultian Subjects," she isolates Foucault's regime of truth, which "offers a framework for the scene of recognition, delineating who will qualify as a subject of recognition and offering available forms for the act of recognition" (Butler, 2005, P.23). This, she contends of his work, acts always in a 'relation to this regime, a mode of self-crafting that takes place in the context of the norms at issue, and, specifically, negotiates an answer to the question of who the "I" will be in relation to the norms" (Butler, 2005, P.23). Further interplay brings forth her two questions, who or what are these norms, and who or what creates the subject, or has a dominion to recognize me as a subject?

Is any kind of representation avoidable, even when giving an account of oneself? "If I try to give an account of myself," Judith Butler states,

...if I try to make myself recognizable and understandable, then I might begin with narrative account of my life. But this narrative will be disoriented by what is not mine, or not mine alone. And I will, to some degree, have to make myself substitutable in order to make myself recognizable (Butler, 2005, P. 37).

Nietzsche moved his philosophy past who am I, to who are we—recognizing the plurality of identities, while Jean-Luc Nancy's conception of singular-plural served, in keeping with Michael Anker's work, as an amendment to the Heideggarian *being-with.* (Anker, 2009, P. 16)

Schirmacher's work gives a more precise account of *being-with-technology* and bodily living through homo generator, and his thoughts on the subject in the face of *body politics.*

Homo generator's body politics is to SEE/ HEAR/ SMELL/ TOUCH/ TASTE/ THINK before you act, it claims aesthetic perception as the basis of comprehending and interaction. Homo generator has no fear of his mistakes, for they are inseparable from his succeeding - as body politics teaches us, "Homo generator is a concrete beginning, unique but not original, self care without egoism" (Schirmacher, 1991).

In bridging ideas of representation, the sexual aesthetic, the demarcations of gender, of artificial life and cybernetics, Wolfgang Schirmacher's philosophy of homo generator remains the strong fulcrum—an aporetic nexus. Schirmacher negates our "capacities for reason and compensation all belong without a doubt to the full man" as being a priori or fundamental.

Conclusion: Bodily Living in the Cyber-Realm as a Sexual Being

The homo generator self creates, is always becoming-other, and moves through fluidity in openness. Manufacturing is part of the picture, as is technological artifact, but not the entirety of it. Regarded phenomenologically, the body is free to realize its own ability (and failure), and all the materials of the world merely express its potential (Schirmacher, 1991).

Consider the arrival of the I-Bod. I-Bod is a device that attaches to the IPOD mp3 player. The device vibrates to the beat of the particular song playing, and although the innovators (Simon, 2006) contend that its primary purpose is to increase cardio and respiratory rates, as an assist in exercise, it has found a new purpose—namely, as a sexual enhancement device, akin to a vibrator. In this case, the technology is in fact the realization of the electronic orgasm. The web site, OHMIBOD.com, markets the IBOD purely as "The classic style vibrator that syncs with your iPod."
This technology, much like the image of Hammer on her bed with an electronic stimulator, is in no way a *negation* of the body, body tactility, or bodily living. As Schirmacher states,

> The revolution of the artifacts is perceived as a negation of the natural body. Dolls function as an inscription of the body, bear our consent to the abstraction game which has been going on for quite some time now. Our culture is fascinated with the immaterial body which knows no aging process and may overcome even death. (Schirmacher, 1994)

If we experience life, in part, through aesthetics, and are called upon as homo generator in the being-becoming-creating paradigm, Barbara Hammer's image of sexual identity aesthetic, as portrayed in *No Nooky TV* gives a most immediate implementation of *homo generator aesthetics*. The self creating, the self loving, the relationship to unseen other, to creation of self through the particl-d minoritarian, to the encapsulating being of the Nietzschean *I* and *we*, through bodily living. Or, as Barbara Hammer states, "A lesbian film artist births herself" (Hammer, 2010, P.99).

Bodily living in the *cyber-realm* means understanding that each word, each shock, each pang is tactile—emotionally, physically. The body/mind responds to the stimuli in the perpendicular. Bodily living in the cyber-realm is the ever presence of being 'turned on,' not limiting this phrase to sexual arousal, but a total 'on state,' acute biological reflexes. This is not, then, a bodiless interaction. The tactility of sexuality is ever present in our cyber bodies, whether it comes from one hand on the mouse, virtual reality, or diodes, we are indeed experiencing a physical response in our physical bodies to the impetus in cyber-space, or in the *studium* and *punctum* of aesthetics. As Wolfgang Schirmacher states, "Our cyberbody is neither a prosthesis nor does it limit the imagination, but it is a particular medium of our intercourse with the world and our technological 'being for the world' (Deleuze)" (Schirmacher, 1991). Put more succinctly, "(the) human body awareness is nowhere needed and used more than in surfing the internet" (Schirmacher, 1994).

The apoesies in militant technology and aesthetics is crucial for understanding the self as a sexual being, whose multiplicity in identity (including sexual identity) require no commodification by corporate interests, even those stemming from the adult entertainment industry. It requires sovereignty in the account of oneself through just living and aesthetic function. Homo generator is living. Aesthetics is the experience of life.

Chapter Seven: On the Aesthetics of Homo Generator in the Singularity

Homo Generator And Living Artfully as Artifact
On Carolee Schneeman
Homo Generator and the Aesthetics of Human Transcendence
Homo Generator in The Coming Singularity

> *The work of art exists only in relation to the individual who contemplates or produces it*
>
> —Theodore Adorno, 2007, P. 250

> *But the post-Singularity world _does_ fit with the larger tradition of change and cooperation that started long ago (perhaps even before the rise of biological life). I think there _are_ notions of ethics that would apply in such an era. … And while mind and self will be vastly more labile than in the past, much of what we value (knowledge, memory, thought) need never be lost. I think Freeman Dyson has it right when he says [9]: "God is what mind becomes when it has passed beyond the scale of our comprehension.*
>
> —Vinge

In his essay "Singularities and Nightmares" theorist and science fiction writer David Brin offers four options of how the Coming Singularity may play out. The four broad categories are:

1. **Self-destruction.** Here he offers different forms of self-destruction from social collapse to what he calls "ecological suicide."

2. **Positive Singularity** — or, as he states, a "phase shift to a higher and more knowledgeable society." In general, this would democratize our understanding of technology and would move human understanding to a new evolution of living through technology. This is a sincere outlook on the possibility of human self-improvement.

3. **Negative Singularity** — this is the *Terminator* or *Matrix* version of the singularity—the self aware technological system that destroys the human race as an invasive virus. This form of self actualization is the fodder of many post-apocalyptic novels and films.

4. **Retreat** --This scenario is the embrace of the neo-luddite. Specifically, the branch of the neo-ludditic understanding that moves away from utilizing technology for cottage industry purposes, and gravitates instead toward a more "human" society that lives in harmony with nature and the natural world. Technology would be all but destroyed, and a strong hierarchy would need to be formed in order to maintain a natural world. Think *Planet of the Apes*, but with humans running things. (Brin)

What happens then when machines become sentient, or at the very least, self aware? Machines have had an element of self-generation for a while, but not in the state of autopoesies, rather at the controls of assembly line workers or manufacturers capable of hitting an 'on' or 'off' switch. When the machine becomes self-aware, and begins creating other machines, how does this homo generator co-exist with the human homo generator? Indeed, as the lines of distinction that separate man and machine intersect and then blur to the point of eradication, is it still an act of homo generation or does this new birth point to hetero generation? While there are some doomsday scenarios that Hollywood still likes to produce that demonstrate technology as the ultimate other, Kurzweil gives reassuring words that such a scenario seems unlikely. Indeed, the first rule to evolution, which has played such a strong role in homo generation (and vice versa), is that in order to survive a species must exist with diversity.

The Coming Singularity, then, is one that offers multiplicity (Deleuze and later Hardt)—hetero generation in the survival of man, machine, hybrid, and the new paradigms post Moore's law. The new paradigm must continue to investigate aesthetics, what we create, how we create, and what artifact and artificial living truly is.

Homo Generator and Living Artfully as Artifact

Wolfgang Schirmacher's theory, Homo Generator, is in large part about bringing the self into the world. The creation of self, the human creation of human, the human use of tools—it is about identity, living in what he calls the Artificial Life, and living artfully or *Just Living*.

While his theory is complex and far reaching, the core concept, that of self creation, goes to the heart of the Sovereign Cyber-Netizen.

Schirmacher asks, "Do we construct reality in our heads, is the brain the true creator of humanity and the world?" Where is the world (arti-ficial) located?   The first step for Schirmacher is to locate artificiality, and negate its false meaning, that it has become a pejorative for destructive technology. He argues that the most important connotation is "the proximity to art and autopoiesis" (Schirmacher, 1994).

Over the previous chapters, the discussion has revolved around instances in achievement or negation of sovereignty in the ethical encounter through a series of prisms: that of social

networking on death in the cyber-realm; that of information encounters under the veil of journalism in the cyber realm; through
advancement in curricular studies in ethical encounters outside
of top-heavy corporate machinery. And finally, through art and
aesthetics, and this chapter will further investigate the autopoiesis,
what Heidegger referred to as the simultaneous creation of the
work of art, and the artist herself, through the rendering of art.

It is, in fact, a celebration of plurality in being, of the conflicts
of truth, but also of creation and living through creation, and being with the world (*mitsein*) through creation, the creation of self.
A positive singularity.

In this consideration, one must push for openness and openings, an open circuit and conduit of information, identity, empathy, being-becoming, through striated space. Lisa Nakamura,
in her exploration of *cyber types* suggests, correctly, that we still
hold onto bodily demarcations and identifiers, but these do not
physically have to be fixed in the off line world, if we so choose,
nor do we need to approach bio-technics as a negation of self.
Rather, the self can be augmented, recreated, edited, and created
anew.

In the fusing of these horizons, we are art—we, the human
race, are the art and artifact of creation. This is not to suggest that
we are then devoid of humanity, as Heidegger tells us, "A man is
not a thing" (Heidegger, 2007, P. 184). As artifact, we are still humans living in a culture of self-creation, in autopoiesis, where we
are our own sovereign as homo generator.

Where Adorno saw horror in the manifestation of the culture industry, Homo Generator sees the end of this as a controlling mechanism. Aesthetics self-generates through Dasein. It is impossible
to understand the world without aesthetics. Aesthetics guides
principles of learning, creation, and *being-becoming*. Aesthetics is
the educated and higher expression of understanding in the world.

It is living art-fully (Schirmacher) and having presence in artificial life.

Living artfully, then, in this artificial life calls upon us to move past the limited thinking of barriers, of nation-state sovereignties, of the negative-generation in anti-aesthetics. As Adorno tells us, "Freedom, the presupposition of art and the self-glorifying conception art has of itself, is the cunning of art's reason" (Adorno, 2007, P. 246). Aesthetics is freedom. Living artfully through aesthetics compels us to use technology as a realization of ethical encounters and expression.

When discussing his *Aesthetic Theory*, Theodor Adorno postulated that our experience of art calls upon our experience of nature, and that if something were to be beautiful in art, it was beautiful in nature first. This kind of negotiation is a negative dialectic that is based on a question of premise, and of homo compensator. Indeed, the notion that man is removed from nature, and that technology, the flesh of our flesh, is at odds with the natural world is not a necessary binary opposition. Indeed, aesthetics, were it to have any value, is the aesthetics of homo generator.

In his work, *Eye and Mind*, Merleau-Ponty fuses ontological principles, and pushes existentialism in a direction somewhat dissimilar from Jean-Paul Sartre. Indeed, he looks upon the artist's *being-in-the-world* as a means of rendering *being* visible. "The Painter takes his body with him" (Merleau-Ponty, 2007, P. 289), just as the cyber-netizen takes her body with her through the cyber-realm. The tactility of the body is ever present in the work. To Merleau-Ponty, the body is ever present in the art. "It is by lending his body to the world that the artist changes the world into paintings…that body which is an entwining vision and movement" (Merleau-Ponty, 2007, P. 289).

A person who lives authentically, automatically, and is open, is also open *to*. Open *to* what, precisely? The terrain of examination, which speaks to existence and self creation, is one where the ethical encounters of the sovereign may prevail.

Smooth space (Deleuze and Guattari, 1987, P.384), or nomad space, is that of independent arborescence. In other words, a space that is controlled by flanks, and assigns it "as much as possible a communicational role. (Ibid)" In this space, the striated space of identities overlapping the smooth space of the communication model, it becomes problematic for aesthetic creation. It is a space of uncertainty. As Michael Anker purports, "To make a decision in such a terrain is to decide without the necessities of absolute certainty of absolute knowledge."

An aesthetic space and spatiality then: "Space is in-itself; rather, it is in-itself *par excellence*. Its definition is *to be* in itself (Italics from source). (Merleau-Ponty, 2007, P.295) Yet, even in that space, homo generator "calls attention to the becoming, inventing, and creating nature of being in the world" (Schirmacher).

In the further consideration of this concept, that of the aesthetics of homo generator, the work of multi-media artist Carolee Schneeman, whose key works investigate form and the construction of the artist, will be given some examination.

On Carolee Schneeman

What aesthetics emerge then from autopoiesis, as it is reflected, created, and is as such in artistic creation?   As previously mentioned, Barbara Hammer offers the phrase, "a lesbian filmmaker births herself." On one hand, the statement is formed in conjunction with the notion of reference—if there are no references available for me to pull from, I must then become my own reference. It is also a simultaneous expression of the manifestation of self through living artfully, in the artificial life. Art, artifact, representation, autopoiesis merge in the generation of being-becoming.

Multi-media artist Carolee Schneeman is an artist whose work has courageously showcased aesthetic taboos and traditions, while engaging her own body in relation to the body of a social order. Much of her work has been seen internationally, and she has had several retrospectives as well. Film, performance art, sculpture, painting—she has tried her hand at nearly every available art form in the 20ᵗʰ and 21ˢᵗ centuries. She has also earned a number of prizes and accolades. One of her works begins quite simply with a performance.

Artist Carolee Schneeman stands on a table in East Hampton, NY (and later recreates this at the Telluride Film Festival, Colorado). Schneeman is naked. She begins to paint her body with mud, and then stands with her legs apart. She reaches inside herself, and pulls from her vagina, a scroll that she then reads. This piece of performance art, which she called Interior Scroll, was then captured in photographs and on film. In describing the work, she focused on the womb as a place of birth and creation. "I saw the vagina as a translucent chamber of which the serpent was an outward model" (Schneeman, 2010).

The birthing of the artifact announces her arrival as becoming-artist. The scroll itself, while a product in the formation of the work, becomes art once its use is enacted. The performance evokes Merleau-Ponty's notion of 'metamorphoses of being' (Merleau-Ponty, 2007, P.292). What has changed is the self in being-becoming, as Schneeman becomes the artifact in self-production. While Heidegger suggests that, "The work belongs, as work, uniquely within the realm that is opened up by itself. For the work-being of the work is present in, and only in, such opening up" (Heidegger , 2007, P. 196). Merleau-Ponty pushes against this assertion a bit, "Art is and is not being-for-itself. Without a heterogeneous moment, art cannot achieve autonomy."

But what is the heterogeneous moment? "More than a mere

reversal of Hegel, re-inscribing the heterogeneous articulates a crisis in the basic mechanics of Hegelian dialectics. Without continuity in concepts, sublimation comes to a standstill" (Harding, 1997, P. 25) Then it is a moment in which difference is revealed in the creation of the artifact. "For the imaginary is much nearer to, and much farther away from, the actual—nearer because it is in my body as a diagram of life of the actual" (Merleau-Ponty 2007, P. 291).

In a separate work, Carlolee Scheeman plays with temporality and the expression of lovemaking on the screen. The film, *Fuses*, begins with a series of overlapping and uncertain images. The images, themselves, are strongly erotic. Carolee and her male lover engaged in positioned lovemaking, oral lovemaking, and occasionally are seen clothed in moments of non sexual rapture. There is a dance to the interplay, and moments when the temporality calls attention to itself. Though the lovemaking is real there is an element of simulation on the screen.

"For the film, what matters primarily is that the actor represents himself to the public before the camera rather than representing someone else." (Benjamin) The literal representation is throughout Schneeman's work, and yet it is a simultaneous departure as she is clearly enacting performativity (Butler).

Heidegger interrogated what he called "truth in art" (Heidegger, 2007, P. 199). "The actual reality of the work has been defined by that which is at work in the work, by the happening of truth." Also, he tells us, in the work as well. Moving into craft, and work a craft of truth. "Truth happens only by establishing itself in the conflict and sphere opened up by truth itself. (Heidegger, p. 200) "

Heidegger in *The Origin of the Work of Art* states that "As necessarily as the artist is the origin of the work in a different way than the work is the origin of the artist" (Heidegger, 2007, P. 182). --In other words, the artist becomes artist by producing art, just as art becomes such in its production. Homo Faber, as a category under homo generator, realizes a become-becoming of both work and artist in shared temporality. Homo generator "simultaneously calls attention to the becoming, inventing, and creating nature of being in the world" (Anker, 2009, P. 33).

For Merleau-Ponty, art is a summation of light, color, reflections, "the objects of his quest are not altogether real objects; like ghosts they have only visual existence" (Merleau-Ponty, 2007, P. 292).

Scheeman holds the world in suspension—in the animated love making, in the removal of the scroll from inside. The being-becoming of art and artist in the act of generation though the images play as a means of representation, the real remains visible in the act of creation as creation.   Merleau-Ponty argues that the brute meaning rendered from art is done so in "full innocence."

For Adorno, Art remains at the social "antithesis of a society." Yet, Art needs the artist.   Needs the hands to create, the inspired mind, the artifact needs a producer, even if art itself can be seen as a byproduct of self production, and is constantly influenced by the 'social web of delusion,' even as it acts against it.   Art does not "seek to produce pleasure as an immediate effect."   Barthes in his conceptualization of the *studium* and *punctum* may agree. The immediacy of art is not evident in the first experience of the work. Heidegger offers that art has an 'essential ambiguity and that this element is essential in defining a kind of truth--art as 'the setting-into-work of truth' (Heidegger, 2007, P.210).

In drawing out effects of the work, the viewer behaves external to it, as a judge with a period of deliberation that she may not entirely be aware of. The act of this deliberation is one that places the viewer above the artifact for a moment, as the enactment of a judgment requires (for Arendt) a balanced view of a work. Yet, the work may be one that intentionally provokes the viewer, or ruptures an experience in order to distort an orderly appreciation in judgment. This is an element to Schneeman's work that is present throughout much of her catalogue. By suspending the viewer out of balance, the act of judgment which may engage our desire for a superior nature, becomes almost difficult to achieve outside of a momentary reflex.

This reflex, then, is not the enactment or performance of judgment, but rather a real response to what is immediate—the *studium*. If creation, then, is one in which judgment of the artist is available throughout, how does this then affect the viewer when the viewer (as subject and homo generator) is also an artifact of this artificial life?

What will art require in the singularity?

Homo Generator: The Aesthetics of Human Transcendence

Science and technology are moving toward an age that may make our superhero movies, cartoons, and comic books seem more believable. The world of stories that these characters inhabit are no longer as far-fetched as it may have seemed a generation ago. "It is only now, in the encroaching post-technological epoch, that the immense world-engendering powers of Homo generator become evident." (Schirmacher)

Part of the question remains how the singularity concept interacts with human transcendence—including questions of immortality or at the very least fulfilling a human vitality not seen in previous generations of the species. Human beings, by living artfully through technology and the cyber-realm, are facing a new step for the species—a step beyond the homo sapiens.

Paul Miller (aka DJ Spooky), visiting artist and Professor at the

European Graduate School, makes the following assertion:

> Combine everything from DNA sequencing to robotics to nano-engineering to space flight, and realize that we are embarking on the first steps toward transforming the species. Future generations won't have a "dependence" on technology. They will have technology as a core aspect of their existence" (Miller, 2004, p. 17).

Brin speculates that *opponents* of science and technology clutch their own conceptions of "messianic transformation." That in achieving a kind of technological fluidity in human life, that human beings are somehow negating a spiritual existence, and that there are dire post-life consequences in a metaphysical realm for achieving technological gains here.   Moral behavior or disciplined nature of a kind will be rewarded, while any advancement made outside of these tenets are questionable, ambiguous, or flat out wrong. This kind of thinking will more than likely be short lived, as technological advancements have occurred contemporaneously with the decline of organized spiritual vitality.

The mobility of the human body already in the material world and in the cyber-realm serves as reminders of our place within the world. Bearing witness to one another as evolving beings requires a phenomenological perspective, such as Merleau-Ponty offers.
In the world there is the thing itself, and outside this thing itself there is that other thing which is only reflected light rays and which happens to have an ordered correspondence with the real thing; "there are two individuals then bound together externally by causality" (Merleau-Ponty, 2007, P. 293).
Merleau-Ponty continues, "My mobile body makes a difference in the visible world, being a part of it; that is why I can steer it through the visible. Conversely, it is just as true that vision is attached to movement" (Merleau-Ponty, 2007, P. 289).

But moving through life, moving through the cyber-realm, and moving through our living world does not mean there is no constant, or that history itself should be ignored or left out of the equation. Looking forward also requires taking stock of what has occurred in the past, if nothing more than for reference, or a reassurance of where we currently are, even if the terrain is in a constant shift. The consistency is that the material world exists as such, even as it augments. For Heidegger, "what is constant in a thing, its consistency, lies in the fact that matter stands together with a form. The thing is formed matter" (Heidegger, 2007, P. 186).

If the positive singularity (when fused with Nancy's singular-plural) becomes the most desirable, questions about how much of our bodies we trade in for artificial limbs, organs, or even synapses may lead to questioning if human survival is even achievable? In other words, at what point is the life that we preserve in the quest for immortality even 'human' anymore? Is there a gradient system, or will sentience be the common denominator? If a human augments her own body with the artificial, yet remains sentient, what of the robot that adopts organic characteristics and remains sentient? Is one more 'human' than the next? Will it be decided by creation? There is plenty of room to argue over what type would be beneficial or even desirable, but the question remains—will human beings become obsolete if the artificial life is not embraced?

Homo Generator in the Coming Singularity

Homo Generator in the singularity remains crucial to the sovereignty of the self. Here we find the governing factors for ethical encounters, aesthetic appreciation and rendering, facing the philosophical questions of death, and bearing witness. It requires the phenomenologist stance—reporting at once what one is facing. Nothing more or less.

In *Declaration of the Independence of Cyber Space*, John Barrow argued against government authority in the cyber-realm, giving sixteen paragraphs to support his central thesis that the internet is free, and people are free to be who they are in cyber-space without the coercion of authoritarian aids.

> We have no elected government, nor are we likely to have one, so I address you with no greater authority than that with which liberty itself always speaks. I declare the global social space we are building to be naturally independent of the tyrannies you seek to impose on us. You have no moral right to rule us nor do you possess any methods of enforcement we have true reason to fear......we will create a civilization of the Mind in Cyberspace. May it be more humane and fair than the world your governments have made before. (Barrow)

Cultural critics, such as Lisa Nakamura, have not seen some of the utopian ideas expressed in this doctrine come to fruition, and have therefore made the assertion that the internet—as a space for ethical encounters, has failed.

What Nakamura does not take into consideration, though, is that the cyber-realm (which includes all mediated communication, identity creation, etc.) is a form of virtual Homo Faber in the Homo Generation paradigm. Also, this form of cultural criticism ignores the exponential growth of information and other technologies, which will ultimately be devices we live through. If technology is the flesh of our flesh, and a product of homo generation, and we ourselves are a product of homo generation, then we are an artifact living in what Schirmacher calls the artificial life.

As homo generators living artfully, the coming singularity (as Vinge and Kurzweil have argued) will be the dawn of a new age— the first new age post the industrial revolution in which artificial intelligence achieves sentience, human beings can augment their bodies through nanotechnology, technological advances continue through a three dimensional exponential growth pattern, and humans achieve a transience of a nearly god-like status in the creation of their own artificial worlds.

In investigating what new models may emerge, art and aesthetics remain absolutely invaluable tools that help us translate the emerging world (virtual or otherwise) around us, and a number of artists have already begun imagining the next step in living artificially (Schirmacher).

It is in this terrain of artificial life that human beings may truly achieve sovereignty. While questions of ethical encounters remain, and how as educators we must include thinking beyond basic scholarship of how to enact functional ethical paradigms remains in question, we must be prepared for the next evolution of dasein, even as our Being-Toward-Death may not any longer be our own.

Sovereignty, then, is one in which openness is not invasive, but rather aporos, open, welcoming, like a self governing transit switch that will invite or shield as needed. This model of sovereignty, then, is one already present through homo generator in our artificial lives. The phenomenologist already sees this.

The singularity is not 'coming.' It is already here. Being.

References and Further Reading

Abdunnur, S. (2010) Necessity of Terrorism: Political Evolution and Assimilation. Atropos Press. Dresden; New York.

Adorno, T. (2007 Edition). Aesthetic Theory. Continental Aesthetics. Blackwell Publishing. Massachusetts.

Agamben, Giorgio (2005) The State of Exception. University of Chicago Press.

Arendt, Hannah (1998 Edition). The Human Condition. The University of Chicago Press.
Arendt, Hannah (1994 Edition) Eichmann in Jerusalem: A Report on the Banality of Evil. Penguin Classics.
Arendt, Hannah (1995 Edition) Responsibility and Judgment. Schocken publications. New York.

Badiou, A. and Zizek, S. (2009) Philosophy in the Present. English Edition, Polity Press

Badioiu, A. (2011) Alain Badiou's Open Letter to Jean-Luc Nancy. Retrieved from: http://www.versobooks.com/blogs/463-alain-badious-open-letter-to-jean-luc-nancy

Barthes, R. (1981) Camera Lucida. New York: Hill and Wang

Baudrillard, J. (1987) The Ecstasy of Communication. Retrieved from: http://iris.nyit.edu/~rcody/Thesis/Readings/The%20Ecstacy%20of%20Communication%20-%20Baudrillard.pdf

Baudrilliard, J. (1994) Simulacra and Simulation. Sheila Faria Glaser (Translator). Ann Arbor Press

Barrow, John. Declaration of the Independence of Cyberspace. Retrieved from: http://w2.eff.org/Censorship/Internet_censorship_bills/barlow_0296.declaration

Benjamin, W. (2008 Edition) The Work of Art in the Age of its Technological Reproducibility and Other Writings on Media. The Belknap Press of Harvard University Press. Cambridge, Massachusetts. London, England.

Brandi, J (2010). Bearing Witness. Retrieved from: www.thelittle-rebellion.com

Brin, David. Singularity and Nightmares. Retrieved from: http://lifeboat.com/ex/singularities.and.nightmares#upside

Butler, J. (1995). Melancholy gender—refused identification. Psychoanalytic Dialogues.

Butler, J. (2004). Precarious Life: The Power of Mourning and Violence. Published by Verso.

Butler, J. (2005). Giving an Account of Oneself. Fordham University Press

Butler J., and Agamben G., (2009) Eichmann, Law and Justice. Retrieved from: http://www.youtube.com/watch?v=iC_Kc_IBXlg&p=3FDE396D36A8AC8D&index=6

Carroll, Ed. (2010) Public Lecture given at SUNY New Paltz, April 21st, 2010.

Chomsky, Noam. (2003) Reasons to Fear U.S. Retrieved from: http://www.chomsky.info/articles/20030907.htm

Current.com

Current TV, Pornography Numbers. Retrieved from http://current.com/17opn4c

Deleuze G., (1986) Cinema 1: The Movement Image. University of Minnesota Press.

Deleuze G., Guattarri F., (1972, March 1983 Ed.)Anti-Oedipus. University of Minnesota Press.

Deleuze G., Guattarri F., (March 1987 Edition) A Thousand Plateaus. University of Minnesota Press.

Derogatis, J. (2000) Let It Blurt. The Life and Times of Lester Bangs, America's Greatest Rock Critic. Broadway; Later Printing edition. New York.

Derrida, Jacques (1993) Aporias. Stanford University Press

Di Paolo, E. (2001) Hans Jonas The Phenomenon of Life. Retrieved From http://www.informatics.sussex.ac.uk/users/ezequiel/dipaolo-jonas.pdf

Fisk, Jon (2003). *Act Globally, Think Locally*. PP 227-285. Planet TV. New York University Press. New York and London.

Fitzpatrick, Katherine (2007). If you really liked the reading... Retrieved From http://machines.pomona.edu/149-2007/node/182

Freud, S. (November 1922). Mourning and Melancholia. Journal of Nervous & Mental Disease: Volume 56 - Issue 5 - ppg 543-545. PDF

Garner, J. (2002) Stay Tuned: Television's Unforgettable Moments. Andrews McMeel Publishing. Kansas City.

Hammer, B. (March 2010) Hammer: Making Movies out of Sex and Life. Feminist Press.

Hänggi, Christian (2009). Hospitality in the Age of Media Representation. Atropos Press. New York and Dresden.

Haraway, D. (1991) A Cyborg Manifesto. Retrieved From: http://www.egs.edu/faculty/donna-haraway/articles/donna-haraway-a-cyborg-manifesto/
Haraway, D. (2003). Companion Species Manifesto Lecture 2003. EGSVIDEO You Tube Chanel. Retrieved from: http://www.youtube.com/watch?v=-pHo9dY6KV8

Harding, J. (1997) Adorno and the Writing of the Ruins. The State University of New York. Retrieved from: http://books.google.com/books?id=OT8yfsEUcw8C&printsec=frontcover#v=onepage&q&f=false

Haughstead, L. (2007) Current Tweaks Web Strategy. Retrieved from: http://www.multichannel.com/article/130781-Current_TV_Tweaks_Web_Strategy.php

Heidegger, M. (1982 Edition) The Question Concerning Technology and Other Essays. Harper Perennial Press.

Heidegger, M. (2007 Edition). Being in Time. Continental Aesthetics. Blackwell Publishing. Massachusetts.

Heilscher, M. (2003) German 20th Century Philosophical Writings. Published by Continuum

Holbert, R.; Lambe, J; Dudo, A; and Carlton, K. (March 2007). *Primacy Effects of 'The Daily Show' and National TV News Viewing: Young Viewers, Political Gratifications, and Internal Political Self-Efficacy* Journal of Broadcasting & Electronic Media, Volume 51, Number 1.

Horkheimer, M, and Adorno T. (1969) The Dialectics of Enlightenment. Contiuum Press

Isseks, F. Media courage: Impossible Pedagogy in Artificial Community

Jenkins, N. (2010). Heidegger and the Freedom of Being With. A thousand rhizomes blossoming. Retrieved from: http://athousandrhizomes.wordpress.com/2010/06/25/ heidegger-and-the-freedom-of-being-with/

Karevegan, Jean-Francoise (2000) SOVEREIGNTY AND REPRESENTATION IN HEGEL JEAN-FRANÇOIS KERVÉGAN The Philosophical Forum, Volume 31, Issue 3&4 (p 233-247) Retrieved From: http://onlinelibrary.wiley. com/doi/10.1111/0031-806X.00040/

Kojève, A. (1964) Oeuvres Completes: tome 3, Editions Gallimard, Paris, 1964 p.77

Kroker, A. & Kroker, M (eds.) (1987) Body Invaders, Panic Sex in America. New York: St. Martin's Press.

Kurzweil, Ray. A University for the Coming Singularity (June 2009) Retrieved From: http://blog.ted.com/2009/06/02/ announcing_sing/

Laing, R. (1983) The Politics of Experience, Pantheon Press

Levinas, E. (1998 Edition). Otherwise in Being. Duquense University Press.

Lyotard, Jean-Francois (1993 Edition). Libidinal Economy. Indiana University Press

McLuhan, M (1963) Understanding Media: The Extensions of Man. Signet, The New American Library

Miller, Lisa. (February 16, 2010) Facebook and Death. Newsweek. Retrieved from: http://www.newsweek.com/2010/02/16/r-i-p-on-facebook.html

Milton, J. (1918) Paradise Lost. Retrieved from: http://books. google.com/books?id=9LU6AAAAMAAJ&dq=paradise +lost&printsec=frontcover&source=bn&hl=en&ei=up-fTMOzA8GAlAex99nrCg&sa=X&oi=book_result&ct=res ult&resnum=4&ved=0CDIQ6AEwAw#v=onepage&q&f= false

Moore, Geoffrey (2002). Crossing the Chasm. Harper Paperbacks; Revised edition.

Mulvey, L. (1989) Visual and Other Pleasures. Indiana University Press

Mumford, L. (1963). Technics and Civilization. Manner
    Publications

Nakamura, L (2002) Cyber-Types: Race, Ethnicity, and Identity
    on the Internet. Routledge.

Nancy, Jean-Luc (2011). What the Arab Peoples Signify To Us
    http://www.versobooks.com/blogs/455-what-the-arab-
    peoples-signify-to-us-by-jean-luc-nancy

Gary Peters, "Time to Die: The Temporality of Death and the
    Philosophy of Singularity" from Making Sense of Dying
    and Death Andrew Fagan (ed.) Retrieved from: http://
    books.google.com/books?id=F-RYofDsunoC&printsec=fr
    ontcover#v=onepage&q&f=false

Reed, F. (June 14, 2010) Twitter, Iran, and Reality One Year Later.
    Marketing Pilgrim. Retrieved from: http://www.marke-
    tingpilgrim.com/2010/06/twitter-iran-and-reality-one-
    year-later.html

Sex, Violence, and Profanity in the Media Fact Sheet TV Statistics
    (2010) Parents Television Council. Retrieved From http://
    www.parentstv.org/ptc/facts/mediafacts.asp

Pokin, S. (November 10, 2007) Pokin Around: A Real Story, A Real
    Death.   Retrieved from: http://stcharlesjournal.stltoday.
    com/articles/2007/11/10/news/sj2tn20071110-1111stc_po-
    kin_1.iii.txt

Postman, N. (1992) Technopoly: The Surrender of Culture to
    Technology.

Porn Gives Employee Benefits, Vanguard Documentary Current TV (2010). Retrieved From http://current.com/shows/van-guard/92572706_porn-gives-employee-benefits-scenes-from-vanguard.htm

Rachel Maddow Interviews Jon Stewart Part 1/4. Retrieved from: http://www.youtube.com/watch?v=AkHq_wueVMw

Ranciere, J. (2006) The Politics of Aesthetics. Continuum; Pbk. Ed edition

RICKYBAINS1 (2010) What effect has downloading MP3's affected the Music Industry. Hub Pages. Retrieved from: http://hubpages.com/hub/What-effect-has-downloading-and-mp3s-had-on-the-music-industry

Rixam, R. (2010) Young People Do Not Buy Music Rebuffed. Beats Media. Retrieved From: http://beatsmedia.com/news/1621

Ronell, A. (2009) On Authority. Retrieved from: http://www.egs.edu/index.php?id=27817&part=11

Rosen, J. (July 19, 2010). "The Web Means the End of Forgetting." The New York Times. Retrieved from http://www.nytimes.com/2010/07/25/magazine/25privacy-t2.html?_r=2

Schirmacher, W. (1985) The Faces of Compassion. Retrieved From: http://www.egs.edu/faculty/wolfgang-schirmacher/articles/the-faces-of-compassion/

Schirmacher, W. (1985) Privacy as an Ethical Problem in the Computer Society. Retrieved From: http://www.egs.edu/faculty/wolfgang-schirmacher/articles/privacy-as-an-ethical-problem-in-the-computer-society/

Schirmacher, W. (1991) On The Inability To Recognize the Human Flaw, Just Living Retrieved From http://www.egs.edu/faculty/wolfgang-schirmacher/articles/on-the-inability-to-recognize-the-human-flaw/

Schirmacher, W. (1994) "Homo Generator - Militant Media and Postmodern Technology." In: Gretchen Bender, and Timothy Duckrey. *Culture on the Brink: Ideologies of Technology (Discussions in Contemporary Culture).* The New Press. Pp. 65-79

Schirmacher, W. (1994) "Networld From Within." Retrieved from: http://www.egs.edu/faculty/wolfgang-schirmacher/articles/networld-from-within/

Schirmacher, W. (1994) "Techno Culture and Life Technique." Retrieved from: http://www.egs.edu/faculty/wolfgang-schirmacher/articles/technoculture-and-life-technique/

Schirmacher, W.(2001) Netculture. *Poiesis.* EGS Press. Toronto. No. 3, 2001. Retrieved from http://www.egs.edu/faculty/wolfgang-schirmacher/articles/netculture/

Schirmacher, W. (2003) German 20th Century Philosophical Writings. Published by Continuum

Schirmacher, W. (1989). Media as Lifeworld. Retrieved from: http://www.egs.edu/faculty/wolfgang-schirmacher/articles/media-as-lifeworld/

Schirmacher, W. and Lyotard, J F (2005) Homo Generator in the Postmodern Discussion. From a Conversation with Jean-François Lyotard. Retrieved from: http://www.egs.edu/faculty/wolfgang-schirmacher/articles/homo-generator-in-the-postmodern-discussion/

Schirmacher, W. (Media) Media Aesthetics in Europe. Retrieved from: http://www.egs.edu/faculty/wolfgang-schirmacher/articles/media-aesthetics-in-europe/

Schopenhauer, A. (2008 Edition) The Wisdom of Life and Counsels and Maxims. Dig Reads. Retrieved from: http://books.google.com/books?id=uUAmPoWaoIoC&printsec=frontcover&dq=The+Wisdom+of+Life+and+Counsels+and+Maxims&source=bl&ots=8EqwIgESrK&sig=uUqm7gjDpdooSiV3wHGRfMr3zBo&hl=en&ei=762fTKeqHoGBlAfo2KnwAg&sa=X&oi=book_result&ct=result&resnum=3&ved=0CCIQ6AEwAg#v=onepage&q&f=false

Schneeman (2010). Carolee Scheeman. Retrieved from: http://www.caroleeschneemann.com/interiorscroll.html

Simon, S. (2006) A Perilous Encounter With the IBOD, NPR News. Retrieved from: http://www.npr.org/templates/story/story.php?storyId=5317505

Sites, K. (2005) Retrieved from: *Hotzone.yahoo.com (the site has since been removed)* Redirection retrieved from: http://current.com/1gm324c

Straczynski, J M (1996) The Complete Book of Scriptwriting. Writers Digest Books.

Steinberg, S. (2010). College Students have less empathy than past generations. USA Today. Retrieved from: http://www. usatoday.com/news/education/2010-06-08-empathyre-search08_st_N.htm

Ulmer, G. L. (2003). Internet Invention: From Literacy to Electracy. New York: Longman

Ulmer, G. (2010) Imagining Place: Gregory Ulmer. Retrieved from: http://www.rhizomes.net/issue18/ulmer/index.html

Vinge, Verner. The Coming Singularity. Retrieved from: http:// science.kennesaw.edu/~hmattord/articles/The%20 Coming%20Singularity/The%20Coming%20Singularity. htm

Weber, S. (2010) Politics in the Singularity. Retrieved From ?

Webster, S. (May 4, 2010) Russian paper suggests 'nuclear explo-sion' could cap gulf oil geyser. The Raw Story Retrieved from: http://www.rawstory.com/rs/2010/05/russian-paper-suggests-nuclear-explosion-cut-gulf-oil-geyser/

Will Social Media Save the Sex Industry, Vanguard Documentary Current TV (2010). Retrieved From http://current.com/ shows/vanguard/92572717_will-social-media-save-the-sex-industry-scenes-from-vanguard.htm

Zizek, S. (2010).   First as Tragedy Then as Farce. Retrieved   from   http://www.youtube.com/ watch?v=cvakA-DF6Hc&feature=channel

Zizek, S (2005).   Interrogating the Real.

Zizek, S. (2006) EGS Interview Part One.   Retrieved from: www.
youtube.com/egsvideo

Zizek, S.   (2002) Welcome to the Desert of the Real.   Verso
Publications. New York and London.

CPSIA information can be obtained at www.ICGtesting.com
Printed in the USA
LVOW060232010213

318107LV00001B/204/P